Su-33

Russia's Carrier-Borne Strike Fighter

HUGH HARKINS

Copyright © 2019 Hugh Harkins

All rights reserved.

ISBN: 1-903630-88-6
ISBN-13: 978-1-903630-88-4

Su-33

Russia's Carrier-Borne Strike Fighter

© Hugh Harkins 2019

Centurion Publishing
United Kingdom

ISBN 10: 1-903630-88-6
ISBN 13: 978-1-903630-88-4

This volume first published in 2019

The Author is identified as the copyright holder of this work under sections 77 and 78 of the Copyright Designs and Patents Act 1988

Cover design © Centurion Publishing and KDP
Page layout, concept and design © Centurion Publishing

All rights reserved. No part of this publication may be reproduced, stored in a retrieval system, transmitted in any form, or by any means, electronic, mechanical or photocopied, recorded or otherwise, without the written permission of the publisher

The publisher and author would like to thank all organisations and services for their assistance and contributions in the preparation of this volume: Almaz Central Marine Design Bureau (Almaz); Aviation Industry Corporation of China (AVIC); Concern Radio-Electronic Technologies (Kret); GosMKB Vympel; JPSC Nevskoe Design Bureau; JSC Concern Granit-Electron; JSC GTERPC Salut; JSC Novator; JSC RAC MiG; JSC RD&PE Zvezda (Scientific-Production Enterprise 'Zvezda'); JSC Tactical Missiles Corporation (TMC); JSC V. Tikhomirov NIIP, Zhukovsky; KBP Tula; Komsomolsk-on-Amur Aviation Plant (KnAAZ) them. Yu. A. Gagarin (KnAAPO); Ministry of Defence of the Russian Federation (MODRF); PJSC Ilyushin Aviation Complex; PJSC Sukhoi (Sukhoi Aviation Holding Company); PJSC United Aircraft Corporation (UAC); PJSC UEC Saturn; Rosoboronexport; Rostec; Russian Federation Presidential Press and Information Office; TsAGI (Federal State Unitary Enterprise 'Central Aero-Hydrodynamic Institute, named after Professor N.E. Zhukovsky); US Department of Defence (DoD) & DIA; Harkins, H. (2016) *Sukhoi Su-27SM(3)/SKM*, Centurion Publishing, United Kingdom and Harkins, H. (2017) *Russian/Soviet Aircraft Carrier & Carrier Aviation Design & Evolution Volume 2*, Centurion Publishing, United Kingdom

CONTENTS

	INTRODUCTION	vii
1	SUKHOI T-10 to T-10S/SM	1
2	T-10K (Su-33/Su-27K)	15
3	ARMAMENT/STORES OPTIONS	51
4	SYRIAN DEPLOYMENT, 2016-2017	61
5	RETIREMENT OR MODERNISATION	65
6	ADDENDUM	77
7	GLOSSARY	84

INTRODUCTION

The intent of this volume is to detail the Sukhoi Su-33 (Su-27K) fourth generation naval strike fighter aircraft design procured for service aboard the Soviet Union (later Russian Federation) Project 1143.5 Aircraft Carrying Heavy Cruiser, *Admiral of the Fleet of the Soviet Union, Kuznetsov*. The volume covers the evolution of the T-10K, which was developed for service as the Su-33, and the limited updates introduced. All technical information regarding the aircraft, systems and weapons have been provided by the respective designers/developers, as has most of the graphic material, with technical and graphic input from other entities such as the Ministry of Defence of the Russian Federation. Certain elements of text, where pertinent, are taken from the volume 'Sukhoi Su-27SM(3)/SKM' (Harkins, 2016) and 'Russian/Soviet Aircraft Carrier & Carrier Aviation Design & Evolution Volume 2' (Harkins, 2017). No attempt is made to detail the Su-27KUB experimental design or the Chinese Su-33 copy, the Shenyang J-15, which are outside the scope of the volume, although both are referred to in the addendum.

1

SUKHOI T-10 TO T-10S/SM

Introduced to operational service as the Sukhoi Su-27K in the mid-1990's, the Su-33 fleet air defence fighter (allocated the NATO (North (North Atlantic Treaty Organisation) reporting name 'Flanker' D) remains, in 2019, the premier ship-based fixed wing aviation asset in service with the Russian Federation Navy. This position remained extant despite the introduction of the 4th+ generation RAC MiG-29KR/KUBR multifunctional strike fighter to Russian Naval Aviation service in 2016. Speculation was that the fleet of twenty MiG-29KR and four MiG-29KUBR strike fighters had been intended to replace the Su-33 as an aircraft carrier based fighter. However, in 2019, it appears that planning calls for the Su-33 to be retained and possibly put through a life extension/modernisation program.

The design origins of the Su-27K go back to the Sukhoi T-10, which dates back to the early 1970's. Design work had commenced, under the leadership of O.S. Samoilovich, in late 1969 when the Sukhoi OBK (Design Bureau) in the then Soviet Union had initiated studies into concepts for a 4th generation long-range air superiority fighter intended for serve with the Soviet IA-PVO (*Istrebitelnaya Aviatsiya Protivo-Vozdushnoy Obstrany*/Air Defence Force). It had been decided from the onset that the new fighter/interceptor would be optimised for the primary air superiority mission, albeit with a stipulation that a secondary ground attack capability would be incorporated. A number of challenging performance goals were stipulated, including a long operational range and a high level of manoeuvrability, which, combined with modern sensors and weapon systems, would contribute to meeting the requirement that the new fighter should be capable of engaging and defeating the most modern western fighter aircraft then projected – typified by the McDonnell Douglas (later Boeing) F-15 Eagle air superiority fighter developed under the American FX (Fighter Experimental) program (Sukhoi).

Development of the T-10 was authorised on 3 March 1971 (Sukhoi). During the course of 1971-1972, Soviet aviation design houses, P.O. Sukhoi, A.I. Mikoyan and A.S. Yakovlev, studied various concept designs, Sukhoi producing a not insignificant number of these in its drive to produce an aircraft unrivalled in its performance class.

Among the concepts studied was a conventional design featuring an integral body similar to that seen on the American F-15. This lost out to a concept that placed great importance on widely spaced engines hung under the body of the fuselage, the vertical tail planes being positioned on the fuselage area between the main wings and horizontal tail planes. The concept was designed around a highly blended fore-body and high lift ogive wing with LERX (Leading Edge Root Extensions). The non-planner wing design featured variable sweep at the leading edge and 'a small influx at the root' (TsAGI). The initial design for the T-10 was complete by September 1971, submitted for design review in February 1972 and, following the preliminary design review, a number of design revisions were incorporated (Sukhoi). Full-scale development commenced in conjunction with development of a lightweight fighter, which would evolve into the Mikoyan; PFI (Advanced Frontline Fighter) – Project 9 (Sukhoi & RAC MiG). This design bore a superficial resemblance to a scaled down version of the Sukhoi T-10, both the design houses arriving at similar high agility optimised configurations as both utilised data from the same research agency.

Su-33 lifting off the springboard of the *Admiral of the Fleet of the Soviet Union, Kuznetsov*. Kret

During the course of 1972-1973, the T-10 was further redesigned, the changes including increased wing area and fuel capacity. The thrust of the proposed power plant, A.M. Lyulka (UEC Saturn) AL-31F (Article 99), was increased to compensate for increased aircraft weight, allowing retention of the design goals for a high thrust to weight ratio, which would translate to increased acceleration, climb rate and manoeuvrability. The new design changes underwent rigorous test and evaluation, which included testing large-scale wind-tunnel models at the wind tunnel facilities of CAHI, SibNIA and the MAI (Ministry of Aviation Industry) during 1973 and 1974, a change of chief designer on the program being implemented in the former year with the appointment of N.S. Chernyakov (Sukhoi).

Top: The T-10 prototype, T-10-1, in the final assembly hall at Sukhoi OKB in January 1977. Above: The structurally complete T-10-1 fuelling in April 1977 at the KLSU laboratory for testing the AL-21FZAI afterburning turbojets. *Sukhoi*

Detailed design work on the prototype, which retained the in-house designation T-10, commenced in 1975 and a static test unit, designated T-10-0 was built (static tests were completed on 19 September 1978). The design retained much of the initial design features of earlier concepts, being described by Sukhoi as 'an integrated ogive wing configuration, [with] leading-edge root extensions, an all-moving horizontal tail unit mounted on the centre wing section continuation beams and twin [vertical] tail fins mounted on engine nacelles at the airframe stern post' (Sukhoi). The variable engine air intakes were positioned 'either side of the plane's roll axis, and suspended from the centre wing section' to ensure a stable air flow to the engines, even when the aircraft was flying at high AoA (Angle of Attack), an issue of high importance for the design team in their drive to produce an air superiority fighter with unrivalled agility for an aircraft in its performance/weight class (Sukhoi). The configuration was designed to be as compact as possible to reduce weigh in combination with the use of titanium alloys. The undercarriage, a conventional tricycle configuration with single wheel main units and a single wheel nose unit, presented problems for the design team, particularly in regard to allocating space for the main unit bays in the compact design. This problem was solved by introducing bays in what was described as the 'dead air' of the central wing sections, beneath the engine air intake ducts, the retraction process requiring the wheels to be rotated as the units retracted (Sukhoi). There was no dedicated air brake installed, the wing flaps doubling as speed brakes.

The T-10 was designed with inherent lateral instability balanced by an EDCS (Electronic Distance Control System), computerised FBW (Fly-By-Wire) FCS (Flight Control System), the incorporation of which was designed to reduce losses attributed to loss of control and increase the aircraft manoeuvrability in close range air combat. The Soviet Union had pioneered FBW technology with the Sukhoi T-4 intermediate range bomber (cancelled in the 1970's), which conducted its maiden flight on 22 August 1972 (Harkins, 2018). The first American combat aircraft designed with a FBW FCS, the General Dynamics YF-16, conducted its maiden flight on 2 February 1974, followed by the first flight of the European Panavia Tornado prototype (then known as the MRCA (Multi-role Combat Aircraft) on 8 August that year.

T-10-1 circa 1977. UEC Saturn

T-10-1 during its maiden flight on 20 May 1977. Sukhoi

Approval of the T-10 configuration was granted by a decree of the Soviet government on 19 January 1976. Three prototypes (two flight and one ground test) were under construction at Sukhoi's experimental plant at Zhukovsky near Moscow by the time M.P. Simonov was appointed as the programs chief designer in February 1976. The T-10-1 was completed in April 1977 and, under the power of two AL-21FZAI afterburning turbojet engines (interim engine rated at 76.49 kN (16,195 lb.) dry and 109.84 kN in afterburner (thrust may have been in excess of these interim ratings), flew for the first time on 20 May 1977 (pilot, V.S. Ilyushin). No less than twelve flying laboratories (test bed aircraft) were flown to test various systems for the T-10. The conceptual critical design review was passed in October 1977 and the second development aircraft, T-10-2, flew in May 1978, followed by a further two, T-10-3 and T-10-4, in 1979, design leadership passing to A.A. Kolchin in this year. T-10-3 and T-10-4 were powered by AL-31F afterburning turbofan engines developed for the T-10 series production design. Each of these engines were rated at 79.43 kN (17,857 lb.) dry and 122.59 kN (27,558 lb.) with afterburner (Sukhoi).

Following construction of the initial batch of four aircraft a further five, T-10-5, T-10-6, T-10-9, T-10-10 and T-10-11, were built at the Komsomolsk-on-Amur production plant. T-10 development aircraft were accepted for service testing in December 1979. Problems encountered during testing led to a redesign that resulted in the T-10S, to address issues such as controlling weight, reducing drag, increase wing lift and improving roll control. This was necessary as it had become clear that the desired superiority over its western counterparts, in particular the F-15, could not be guaranteed with the original T-10 design. The incomplete T-10-7 development aircraft was now completed as the prototype of the new design, receiving the new designation T-10S-1. In this configuration the aircraft conducted its maiden flight on 20 April 1981 (pilot, V.S. Ilyushin), design leadership of the program passing to A.I. Knysheb that year (Sukhoi).

The T-10-5 is shown carrying inert R-27 and R-73E air to air missiles circa late 1970's. Sukhoi

In the original T-10 design a major problem had been encountered with 'early stall on the wing', resulting in 'the sharp front edge of the profile along the entire span being subjected to shaking', which prohibited certain planned manoeuvres (TsAGI). To counter this, Sukhoi, acting on proposals forwarded by TsAGI (Central Aerodynamic Institute), decided to test, on the T-10S, a new wing of trapezoidal design 'with a root influx' and drooping, or deviating, wing tips (TsAGI). This translated to a new tapered wing with a straight, slatted leading edge flap, flaperon and cropped wingtips, incorporating missile launch rails that doubled as anti-flutter weights. The flaperons and differential tailerons replaced the ailerons of the original T-10 design. It was the changes to the fuselage that were most profound, with a shallower, longer, drooping nose and deeper spine. The twin vertical tail fin configuration of the T-10 was retained, but this was moved outboard from the original position on top of the engine nacelles to booms, which lay alongside the engines. The main undercarriage door mounted air brakes of the T-10 were replaced by a single spine mounted unit similar to that seen on the F-15. The new main undercarriage units were repositioned, as was the nose wheel, which was moved slightly aft. However, even with the design changes, problems were encountered during flight testing, especially with the new wing design; a solution being found in reducing the wing area of the leading-edge slats (Sukhoi).

T-10-17, representative of the T-10S configuration, during testing in the early 1980's. Sukhoi

Over the course of two years TsAGI was instrumental in researching a number of innovations and design traits for the T-10S design, including 'remote control with a stability improvement system, static instability at subsonic speeds, a continuously increasing deflection of the wing socks along the angle of attack, an acute influx on the wing' (TsAGI). Once the design was ready the T-10S-1, as noted above, conducted its maiden flight in 1981.

All Su-27S were powered by a two AL-31F afterburning turbofan engines (above). The Su-27K was powered by the AL-31F3 derivative, which had a slightly higher operating power output. Salut

Russian language graphic with basic English translation in parenthesis: фигура, при которой нос самолета пондимается вверх на 110еуо градусов (на су-27, су-37 - до 180 градусов) по отношению к направлению движения, а затем опускается обратно (a figure in which the nose of the aircraft points up to 110° (on Su-27, Su-37 – up to 180°) in relation to the direction of movement, and then lowers back). Впервые была выполнена в испытательном полете заслуженным лтчиком СССР Игорем Волком. (For the first time it was performed in test flight by the honoured USSR pilot Itchik Igor Volk). Широкой публике кобру продемостировал Виктор Пугачев на международном салоне во французском Ле-Бурже в 1989 году (Cobra was shown to the general public by Vicotr Pugachev at the international show in Le Bourget in 1989).

Su-27S series production aircraft would be powered by a pair of AL-31F turbofan engines first flown on the T-10-3. As serial production of the AL-31F commenced at A.M. Lyulka (UEC Saturn) on 11 May 1984, early serial production Su-27S were powered by development and pre-series production engines (Sukhoi). The AL-31F was rated at 79.43 kN dry and 122.59 kN with afterburner. Available information indicates that the AL-31F has a nine-stage HP (High-Pressure) compressor, a four-stage LP (Low-Pressure) compressor and cooled single-stage HP and LP turbines to the rear of the combustor. The efficient air flow afforded by the combination of engine technology, the aircraft air intake design and computer controlled variable inlet guide-vanes, contributed to the Su-27 high performance, conveying varying degrees of capability to conduct extreme high alpha manoeuvres like the 'Cobra' or Tail Slide, without the engines stalling (Salut & UEC Saturn).

The high thrust to weight ratio of the AL-31F bestowed upon the standard Su-27S a high maximum speed (Mach 2+), unrivalled (for the time) supersonic acceleration, climb rate, and manoeuvrability in certain flight regimes, such as sustained turn rate, for an aircraft in its class. Typical engine life was set at around 3,000 hours and between overhaul, 1,000 hours; reasonable values for a Soviet era fighter aircraft engine. It should be noted that AL-31F engines have been run for thousands of hours over their scheduled life expectancy during bench test runs.

The serial Su-27S emerged with a length of 21.9 m (~71 ft. 10 in), height, 5.9 m (~19 ft. 4 in) and wingspan, 14.70 m (~48 ft. 2.7 in). Normal take-off weight was set at 23400 kg (~51,588 lb.) (Su-27SK) with 2 x R-27R1 (NATO reporting name AA-10 'Alamo'), 2 x R-73 (NATO reporting name AA-11 'Archer') air to air missiles and 5270 kg (~11,618 lb) of internal fuel. Maximum take-off weight was put at 30450 kg (~67,130 lb.) (Su-27SK). The Su-27S/SK could accommodate 5270 kg of fuel at normal load and 9400 kg (~20,724 lb.) at maximum fuel-load. The huge volume of fuel allowed an impressive range to be attained – the Su-27S was capable of flying 1340 km (~832 miles) at sea level armed with 2 x R-27R1 and 2 x R-73 missiles. In the same configuration, range was 3530 km (~7,782 lb.) at upper altitude (Sukhoi). Payload, which could be carried on ten wing and fuselage stations, was, according to Sukhoi data, 4430 kg (~9,767 lb.) (other sources suggest around 6000 kg (~13228 lb.), this being maximum with reduced fuel, while the 4430 kg stated by Sukhoi may be the maximum load carried with maximum fuel). Payload includes the primary armament of R-27 semi-active radar homing and infrared homing air to air missile variants and R-73 infrared guided air to air missiles, as well as unguided air to surface munitions for the secondary air to surface role (Sukhoi).

Although a large heavy fighter design the Su-27S showed itself to have an exceptional performance, in many areas, such as range, climb, manoeuvrability, in particular its high alpha flight performance, being superior to its rivals. The airframe has a +9 g limit that can be over-ridden by switching the limiter off. Maximum level speed is stated as 1400 km/h (~870 mph) at sea level and Mach 2.35 at upper altitude. Climb rate is stated as 19800 meters per minute (~64,960 ft. per minute) at sea level, with an operational ceiling of 18500 m (~60,695 ft.).

The Su-27S would be equipped with a modern (for the 1980's) weapons system based around the RLPK-27 weapon control system. This featured a powerful N001 pulse-Doppler radar that was allocated the NATO reporting name 'Slot Back'. This system had a reported detection range of around 240 km (~149 miles), although designer documentation suggests 150 km (~93 miles) against a fighter size target (Tikhomirov NIIP). The radar could track ten targets simultaneously, but once locked onto a target it could not continue to scan for others.

The N001 radar was complemented by an electro-optical complex consisting of an OEPS-27 Electro-Optical Sighting System; an OLS-27 OLS (Optical Location Station) (Article 36Sh) – IRST (Infra-Red Search and Track) and a LR (Laser Rangefinder), facilitating the detection, tracking and engagement of targets passively without the need for radar, the emissions of which betray the host aircraft position. The OLS was located forward of the windscreen, centred. A Shchel HPS (Helmet Pointing System), progenitor to the twenty first century HMTDS (Helmet Mounted Target Designation Systems), allowed engagements of off-boresight targets at angles of up to 60° by cueing sensors – the missile tracker head – onto targets that had not been bore-sighted.

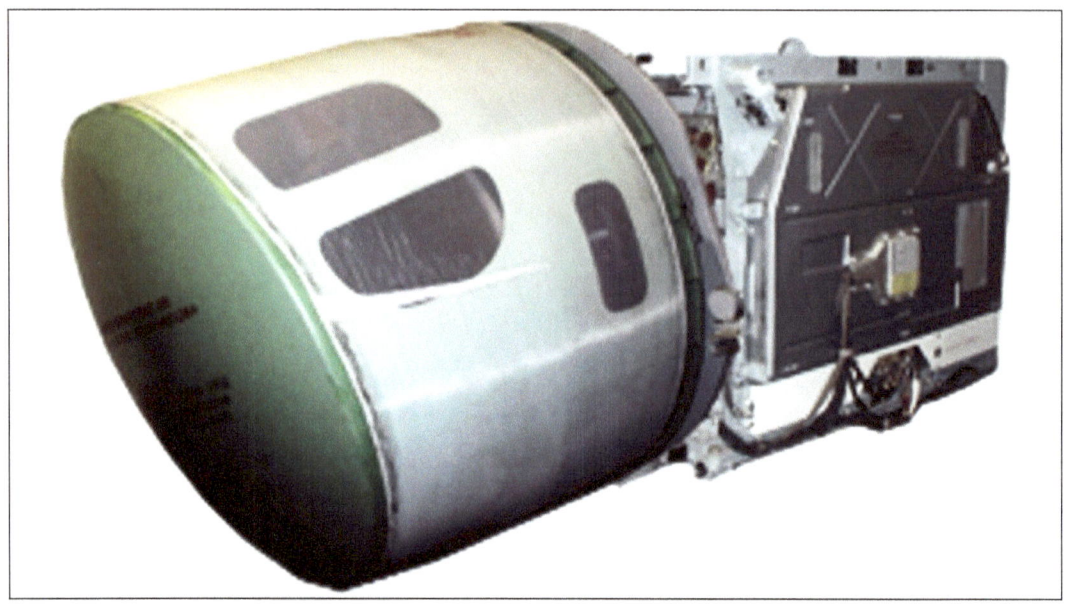

Top: The RLPK-27 weapon control system incorporated a high power N001 radar. Above: The Su-27S cockpit, as would be the case for the Su-27K, was typical of an early 1980's technology design with a plethora of dials and gauges and a central control stick. There was a simple screen for the repetition of sensor data for the pilot who was seated on a K36D zero zero ejection seat. Kret

When NATO aircraft began encountering the Su-27 from the mid-1980's it was noted that the aircraft carried new generation air to air missiles which emerged as the R-27 (Р-27). The R-27 was produced in semi-active radar homing, infrared homing and radiation homing variants. US DoD

MODRF Su-27S Russian language infographic depicting the basic dimensions, Масса пустого (Mass, empty): 17500 kg; Максимальная скорость (Maximum speed): 2125 km/h; дальность полета (range of flight): 3000 km and экипаж (Crew): 2 (for Su-27UB) – Crew for the Su-27S was 1

As well as serving with the Soviet and later Russian Federation air forces, the Su-27 is operated in small numbers in Russian Naval Aviation. This Su-27S, in company with a Su-24M, is serving with Naval Aviation of the Russian Federation Baltic Fleet. MODRF

Once the design of the new fighter was finalised the Su-27S entered series production and the first such aircraft, manufactured at KnAAPO (Komsomolsk-on-Amur Aviation Plant), conducted its maiden flight on 1 June 1982 (conflicting Sukhoi documentation states the additional dates of 2 and 3 June), piloted by Sukhoi test pilot A.N. Isakov (Sukhoi). State Joint Tests commenced on 10 August 1983, stage LKI was completed on 21 August that year with the full test series completed on 18 January 1984 (Sukhoi) (conflicting Sukhoi documentation states December 1983 as the completion date), confirmed the designs expected flight performance superiority over its rivals. This paved the way for service entry, which occurred on 17 June 1985, with the 60th IAP-PVO FAR (Fighter Aircraft Regiment), although the first Su-27S did not actually arrive on 60th IAP-PVO FAR strength until 22 June that year (Sukhoi). Although having been in service for over five years the Su-27S was officially signed into service by a decree of the Soviet government dated 23 August 1990 (confirmed in KnAAPO documentation, but conflicting PJSC Aviation Holding Company Sukhoi documentation states 26 August 1990) (Sukhoi). Following its introduction to service with the air forces of the Soviet Union in June 1985, production continued, with in excess of 500 Su-27's thought to have been produced by the time the Soviet Union was dissolved into a Commonwealth of Independent States on 25 December 1991. Following this dissolution of the Soviet Union, the Su-27 remained in service in the new Russian state, assuming greater importance as older aircraft were designs retired. It is estimated that around 300 Su-

27's remained in service in the Russia Federation in the mid-2010's. Smaller numbers of Su-27's equipped the air forces of some former Soviet Republics and new build aircraft were exported to China, Vietnam and Indonesia, while surplus aircraft were exported to several other nations.

Previous page: Su-27SM1 (top) and T-10M (bottom). A Russian Federation Aerospace Forces Su-27 taxiing for take-off at a snow covered ZVO airfield on 26 January 2019. Rostec/Sukhoi/MODRF

The basic Su-27S airframe spawned a number of variants, including the Su-27UB two-seat operational conversion trainer, the prototype of which, T-10U-1, conducted its maiden flight in 1985 (pilot, N.F. Sadovnikov) and State Joint Tests commenced on 24 May 1986 (Sukhoi). Other derivatives of the Su-27, other than the Su-27K, included the Su-27M, the prototype of which conducted its maiden flight on 28 June 1988 (pilot, O.G. Choi) (Sukhoi). After several prototypes were built, the T-10M-9 serial production model conducted its maiden flight on 21 July 1992 (pilot, F.I. Grigoriev), but the program was terminated in the early 2000's; Su-30M, which led to the multifunctional Su-30MKI/SM and Su-30MK/2 families (the Su-30MK/2 family also incorporated much of the design work conducted for the single-seat Su-27M); the Su-34 multifunctional strike fighter (the prototype, T-10V-1, conducted its maiden flight on 26 July 1990 (pilot, A.A. Ivanov) and the 4th++ generation Su-35S multidimensional super-manoeuvrable fighter, which entered service in 2014. Small numbers of the basic Su-27S were put through a modest modernisation program in the early 2000's, leading to the new build Su-27SM(3), twelve of which were manufactured in the first half of the second decade of the twenty first century. In the decade prior to this, several batches of modernised Su-27S were re-delivered to the Russian Federation Air Force as Su-27SM2/3 series commencing with the first Su-27SM1, which had conducted its post modernisation maiden flight on 27 December 2002 (pilot, E.I. Frolov) (Sukhoi).

2

T-10K (SU-33/SU-27K)

From the earliest days of the T-10 program it had been planned to undertake development of a naval variant of the aircraft for service on the Soviet Union's planned fleet of CTOL (Conventional Take-Off and Landing) capable aircraft carriers. This naval variant would emerge as the T-10K designed as a naval air superiority fighter for service operating from Project 1143.5 ACHC (Aircraft Carrying Heavy Cruiser) deck in the last decade of the twentieth century and the first few decades of the twenty first century.

The road that would lead to a naval variant of the Sukhoi T-10 had begun in 1971 when Sukhoi Design Bureau commenced conceptual design work on the T-10K, which, was then intended to be a naval specific variant of the original T-10 design. Through the decade of the 1970's, efforts were focused on a design capable of operating from a CTOL aircraft carrier design that would utilise steam catapults for assisted take-off and an arrestor to assist high sink rate landing (Sukhoi, Nevskoe DB & Harkins, 2017). With the cancellation of the Project 1153 nuclear powered aircraft carrier program in 1978, the unrealised Sukhoi naval T-10 program went into a period of limbo that extended into 1982 when the program was revived to provide a revamped T-10K that could operate from the projected Project 1143.5 ACHC. This new T01K design would be based on the T-10S air superiority fighter configuration, but with a strengthened undercarriage, wing folding to facilitate storage in the aircraft carrier hanger and a host of other naval specific features, such as incorporation of an arrestor hook for wire arrested landings (Sukhoi).

The Project 1143.5 to 1143.8, intended to supplement and then replace the fleet of four Project 1143-1143.4 HACC (Heavy Aircraft Carrying Cruiser) in Soviet naval service, omitted the steam catapult launch concept in favour of a springboard (ski-jump) ramp. While the springboard concept was more commonly associated with STOVL (Short-Take-Off Vertical Landing) aircraft the Project 1143.5 series were intended from the outset to operate CTOL fixed wing aircraft as well as the possibility of operating a new generation supersonic STOVL fighter in the guise of the Yakovlev Yak-41(141). In addition, the new design would retain the primary

ASW (Anti-Submarine Warfare) role carried over from the Project 1143-1143.4, for which they would operate ASW helicopters as a major element of the embarked air group, along with a handful of helicopters tasked with search and rescue and airborne radar picket – AEW (Airborne Early Warning) roles (Harkins, 2017).

An Su-33 overflies the Northern Fleet airbase at Severomorsk-3, circa 2017. MODRF

In 1976, when the Project 1153 nuclear powered aircraft carrier program was still at the fore of Soviet naval planning, plans were being formulated to address the question of facilities for development and training of a conventional fixed wing naval aviation unit for ship deck operations. A decree of the Soviet government was issued that year for the development of the Soviet naval airfield at Saki in Soviet Crimea, with construction of a naval aviation training complex NIUTK (NITKA) system designed at Nevsky PKB. Development of the training facility at Saki was conducted in cooperation with the Black Sea Shipyard, Proletarian Plant, under the supervision of Nevsky PKB's Y.D. Setgeev (Harkins, 2017).

Top: Yak-38M STOVL fighter and its intended replacement, the Yak-41 (141) supersonic STOVL fighter that lost out to the Su-27 for a place aboard the Project 1143.5 ACHC. Above: Artist rendering of a hypothetical Soviet through deck aircraft carrier with Yak-36M and Yak-41 fighter aircraft on deck. MODRF/DIA

At the heart of the training complex was the installation of the springboard ramp, which allowed development examples of the 4th generation Soviet fighter aircraft, the Sukhoi Su-27 air superiority fighter and the Mikoyan MiG-29 frontal fighter, to conduct ramp assisted take-offs from August 1982. These tests would confirm the systems suitability in assisting the take-off of conventional fixed wing aircraft from the flight deck of the planned Project 1143.5 ACHC, which, as noted above, had superseded the Project 1153.

The third T-10 development aircraft, T-10-3, conducted the first springboard assisted take-off at Saki, Crimea, on 28 August 1982. Sukhoi

To validate the springboard concept, Sukhoi and Mikoyan respectively adapted fourth generation fighter development aircraft to test the technique. Sukhoi conducted a series of springboard tests with the third T-10 development aircraft, T-10-3 (the T-10-3 had conducted its maiden flight powered by AL-31F engines on 26 August 1979) (Sukhoi), during 1982 and 1983. Sukhoi Design Bureau chief test pilot for the naval T-10 program, N.F. Sadovnikov, conducted the first T-10-3 assisted take-off using the springboard at Saki on 28 August 1982, four days before the Soviet Union's Tbilisi Class (Project 1143.5) ACHC was laid down.

On 18 April 1984, a decree of the Soviet government authorised development of the T-10K (Su-27K) under chief designer K.Kh. Marbashev and OKB Sukhoi General Designer M.P. Simonov (Sukhoi), for service on the projected Project 1143.5 ACHC. This followed on from a similar decree issued a short time prior authorising development of a naval variant of the MiG-29, designated MiG-29K. It was unclear at that time, and for several years thereafter, whether or not the two designs were in competition with each other or were to be considered complementary to each other.

A second development aircraft, T-10-25, which was more representative of the T-10S configuration developed for service with the Soviet Air Forces, joined the T-10K development program in 1984 – this aircraft conducted its maiden flight in support of the T-10K program on 3 August that year (pilot, N.F. Sadovnikov) (Sukhoi). The T-10-25, configured for testing the 'structural elements' of the Su-27K (Sukhoi) enabled a series of tests to be conducted on development of the procedure for landing the naval T-10 without leveling off, as well as take-off testing from a new design of springboard ramp, raised to a higher angle. The first so called naval specific landing procedure, whereby the aircraft would touch down on an 'aerofinisher' – dummy aircraft carrier deck – was conducted at Saki, Crimea, on 30 August 1984 (pilot, V.G. Pugachev) (Sukhoi). The first ground based springboard assisted take off with the T-10-25 was conducted on 3 September 1984 (pilot, N.F. Sadovnikov).

Once the T-10U (Su-27UB) two-seat operational conversion trainer program was advancing in the second half of the 1980's, the T-10U-2 was employed on springboard take-off tests at Saki (Sukhoi), fuelling speculation concerning a naval variant of the Su-27UB, which would prove unfounded.

Top: The second T-10U (Su-27UB-2) conducting a springboard assisted take-off at Saki, Crimea. Above: Wind-tunnel model of the T-10K undergoing testing at TsAGI Sukhoi/TsAGI

The T-10-24 canard triplane development aircraft conducted its maiden flight in May 1985. Sukhoi

For the T-10K (Su-27K) and T-10M (Su-27M), Sukhoi adopted what became known as the 'canard tri-plane' configuration. This retained the rear all-moving horizontal tail planes, but added all-moving active canard fore-planes just ahead of the main wing where the fuselage and wing join. The canard system, design of which had commenced in 1977, was studied by Sukhoi as a means of increasing the Su-27s take-off performance and approach characteristics, such as speed, as well as increasing the designs already impressive manoeuvrability, this latter point being very much a secondary consideration (Sukhoi).

The maiden flight of the T-10-24, the first T-10 variant to be equipped with canards, took place in May 1985, by which time the aircraft had also been fitted with production standard vertical tail fins, featuring the cropped fin tops. Although used to conduct tests with a land based springboard at Saki, the T-10-24 lacked essential equipment for the naval role, restricting it to land based operations (Sukhoi) – this was not a problem for the T-10K development program as the Project 1143.5 ACHC would not be available for several years after initiation of the T-10-24 flight test phase in support of the overall T-10K program.

Although initially associated with development of the T-10K and T-10M, the T-10-24 was effectively used to prove the capability of the canards for all the canard tri-plane equipped members of the extended Su-27 family, including the Su-27IB (Su-34), Su-30MKI/SM and the Su-33KUB, all of which, unlike the Su-27K, featured a digital-fly-by-wire flight control systems (the Su-27M also featured a digital FBW FCS).

An early application for the canard-triplane configuration beyond the T-10K was the T-10V (T-10B), developed into the Su-34 multifunctional strike fighter. The T-10V-1 prototype (top) conducted its maiden flight on 13 April 1990. This aircraft undertook a test phase on approach to the Project 1143.5 ACHC fuelling unfounded speculation that this aircraft was the prototype of a two-seat naval conversions trainer for the Su-27K. The Su-37 (Su-27M2) adopted the canard-triplane configuration, flying in this guise in 1996. Sukhoi

The most successful application for the canard triplane configuration, in terms of numbers built, is the Su-30MKI/SM series, which entered flight test in the guise of the Su-30I (top) on 1 July 1997. Above: The first T-10 variant to be equipped with all-moving canard fore-planes, the T-10-24, which conducted its maiden flight in May 1985, was employed on T-10K development work, including conducting springboard assisted take-off's at Saki, Crimea, to test the canard's in this surface/flight environment. The land based canard-triplane configurations improved take-off and landing performance and increased manoeuvrability. Sukhoi

Top: Prior to completion of the T-10K-1 prototype, Sukhoi built the T10K full-scale engineering mock-up used to prove the technology involved in production and operation of the wing and tail folding mechanisms. Designated T-10K-20KTM and adorned with side code Blue 20, this unit, which was completed in 1986, retained the single wheel forward undercarriage unit of the Su-27S. Above: This photograph of T-10K-1 apparently shows the aircraft in the Sukhoi assembly hall in 1987, but it is also, apparently erroneously, stated by Sukhoi as being on a test stand at Saki,. Sukhoi

Previous page and this page top: Following final assembly in the assembly hall at Sukhoi OBK's facility near Moscow in 1987, the T-10K prototype, T-10K-1 (T-10-37), with the side code Blue 37, conducted its maiden flight on 17 August 1987. This page bottom: The Su-27K-1 was utilised in a springboard assisted take-off test phase at Saki, Crimea. Sukhoi

The T-10-24 was followed by a prototype of the Su-27K naval fighter, T-10K-1 (also known as the T-10-37 – the 37 denoted the aircraft side code), which received the designation Su-27K-1. This aircraft, which was built in 1986-87, was the first Su-27 to feature aircraft carrier operating equipment. Simultaneously with construction of the T-10K-1, Sukhoi OKB built a full-scale engineering mock-up of the T-10K to aid development of and test the operation of the wing and tail folding mechanisms. This unit, which was completed in 1986, received the designation T-10K-20KTM and was adorned with the side code Blue 20 (Sukhoi).

The T-10K-1, which conducted its maiden flight on 17 August 1987 (pilot, V.G. Pugachev), was equipped with canard fore-planes that could deflect +7° to -70°, an arrestor-hook, and a retraceable in-flight refuelling probe on the port side forward fuselage to the fore of the cockpit section. This latter point necessitated the OEPS-27 ball, which occupied the central position just ahead of the windscreen on the Su-27S, being offset to starboard (Sukhoi). The wing of the T-10K-1 was an unmodified Su-27S wing, although it was later modified to incorporate a new two section double-slotted trailing-edge flap with drooping ailerons. The ailerons, which were not fitted to any other Su-27 derivative, conferred better roll control on approach, an important trait for an aircraft designed to operate from an aircraft carrier deck. The T-10K introduced strengthened undercarriage units to compensate for the increased stresses encountered during the high sink rate landings associated with aircraft carrier operations. The single front wheel unit of the Su-27S was replaced with a twin wheel unit, also adopted by some later derivatives of the Su-27. A derivative of the Lyulka (UEC Saturn) AL-31F afterburning turbofan engine employed by the Su-27S was selected to power the Su-27K, each of the two of this variant, designated AL-31F3 Series 3, being rated at 12500 kg -2% with afterburner (Sukhoi).

The T-10K-2 (Su-27K-2) conducted take-off and landing trials on the Project 1143.5 ACHC in November 1989. Sukhoi

The second Su-27K prototype, Su-27K-2 ((T-10K-2), was flown on 22 December 1987 (pilot, N.F. Sadovnikov). This aircraft, like subsequent Su-27K's, featured folding wings and folding tail planes that had been demonstrated on the Su-27K full-scale engineering mock-up, T-10K-20KTM, in 1986 (Sukhoi). It was the T-10K-2 that conducted the deck trials aboard the Project 1143.5 in November 1989. Test pilot V.G. Pugachev, then lead test pilot on the Su-27K development program, conducted the first Soviet conventional landing on an aircraft carrier when he landed the Su-27K-2 on the *Tbilisi* (later *Admiral of the Fleet of the Soviet Union, Kuznetsov*) on 1 November 1989 (Sukhoi). MODRF documentation states the date as 21 November (MODRF), but this was in fact the date that the T-10K-2 conducted the first night time landing aboard the aircraft carrier (pilot, Pugachev) (Sukhoi).

Top: Three-view general arrangement drawing of the Su-33 (Su-27K). Above: An Su-27K, circa 1996. Sukhoi/US DoD

Su-33 (Su-27K) Russian Language infographic with English translation in parenthesis (MODRF): Предназначен Для противовоздушной обороны корабельного авианосного соединения, обеспечения действийк других видов авиации ВМФ, ведения воздушной разведки. (Intended for air defence of an aircraft carrier, ensuring the operation of other types of naval aviation, conducting air reconnaissance)

Двигатели (Engines): AL-31F(3) [x 2]

Масса пустого (Mass, empty): 19600 kg

Максимальная скорость (Maximum speed): 2300 km/h

дальность полета (range of flight): 3000 km

зкипаж (Crew): 1

[Basic dimensions should read height, 5.9 m; span, 14.7 m and length, 21.9 m. The two-view general arrangement in the graphic appears to be representative of that for the Su-34 and should, along with the two-view general arrangement drawing dimensions, be disregarded]

Вооружечне (Armament)

Пушечное (Cannon): 1 x 30 мм пушка ГШ-30-1 (боезапас 150 снарядов) (1 x 30 mm gun GSh-30-1 (150 rounds of ammunition)

Неуправляемые ракеты (Unguided rockets): 80 (4 x 20) x 80 мм С-8КОМ/Ц-8БМ в Блоках Б-8М1 или (80 (4 x 20) x 80 mm S-80KOM/Ts-8BM in Blocks B8M1)

20 (4 x 5) x 122 мм С-13Т в Блоках Б-13л или (20 (4 x 5) x 122 mm S-13T in Block B-13L)

4 x 266 мм С-25-ОФМ-ПУ (4 x 266 mm S-25-OFM-PU)

бомбы: свободнопадающие раЗличного назначения, бомбо-вые кассеты (bombs, free fall for various purposes): 8 x 500 кг (фаб-500, рбк-500, 3б-500) или (8 x 500 kg (FAB-500, RBK-500, 3B-500); 28 x 250 кг (фаб-250, рбк-250 И Т.Д.) ИЛИ, 3б-500) или (28 x 250 kg (FAB-250, RBK-250 T.D. or 3B-500); 32 x 100 кг (32 x 100 kg) bombs

УРВВ (URVV) [guided air to air missiles]: 2 x Р-73 (2 x R-73); 4-6 x Р-27Р/ЭР (4-6 x R-27R/ER[1]) 2 x Р-27Т/ЭТ (2 x R-27T/TE[1])

УРВП (URVP) [air to surface missiles]: Х-41 Москит (X-41 Mosquito [Moskit]); П-800 Оникс (P-800 Onyx)

Su-33

Previous page: Front on aspect view of Su-27K (Su-33) on the deck of the *Admiral of the Fleet of the Soviet Union, Kuznetsov* (top) and rear on aspect view (bottom). This page: Front on aspect view of the Su-27K (Su-33). This page (bottom). Su-33 with canards deflected at ~90° to the horizontal. Sukhoi

The Su-27K (Su-33) featured a strengthened undercarriage to absorb high sink rate landings associated with aircraft carrier operations. The Su-27S single nose wheel unit was replaced with a twin nose wheel unit. In the landing approach (above) the Su-27K (Su-33) aligns itself with the centre of the carrier deck, approaching the stern at a flight speed of 240 km/h and a sink rate of ~5 m/s. Sukhoi

Su-33

Page 32: Su-27K (Su-33) main undercarriage units constrained by deck blocks (top) preparing for deck launch (centre) and operating from land base (bottom). Page 33: The Su-33 take-off run on the Project 1143.5 is 105 m. This page: The typical Su-33 assisted landing distance on the Project 1143.5 is 90 m. MODRF/Sukhoi

Top: A Su-33 (Su-27K) approaches for a wire assisted landing at Saki, Crimea. Above: A Su-33, with arrestor hook deployed, approaches for landing on the Project 1143.5 ACHC *Admiral of the Fleet of the Soviet Union, Kuznetsov*. MODRF

Top: Su-33 Red 62 takes the wire with its arrestor hook as it lands aboard the Project 1143.5 ACHC *Admiral of the fleet of the Soviet Union, Kuznetsov*. Above: When not deployed for use the Su-33 arrestor hook is stowed beneath the extended tail cone at the aircraft extreme rear. Sukhoi/MODRF

Top: A Su-33 during operations in the vicinity of the Northern Fleet air base at Severomorsk-3 in Northern Russia. Above: A Su-33 lands at a snow covered Severomorsk-3 with the large slab type air-brake deployed. MODRF

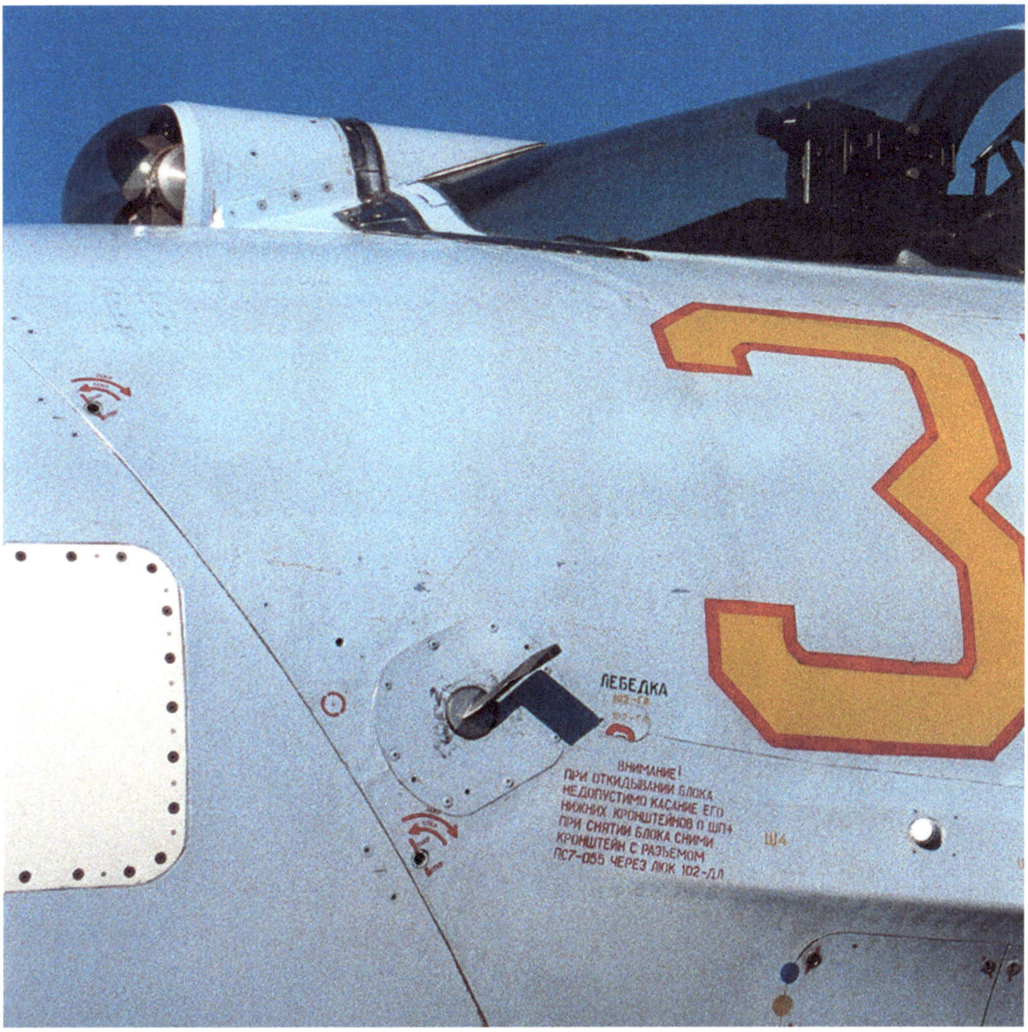
3
ЛЕБЕДКА
ВНИМАНИЕ!
ПРИ ОТКИДЫВАНИИ БЛОКА
НЕДОПУСТИМО КАСАНИЕ ЕГО
НИЖНИХ КРОНШТЕЙНОВ О ШП4
ПРИ СНЯТИИ БЛОКА СНИМИ
КРОНШТЕЙН С РАЗЪЕМОМ
ПС7-055 ЧЕРЕЗ ЛЮК 102-ДЛ
Ш4

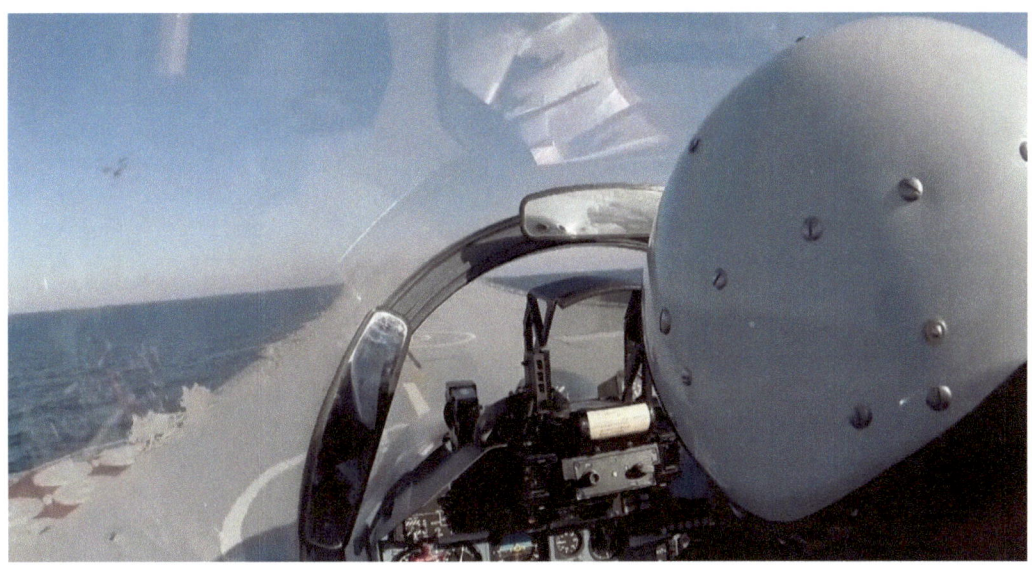

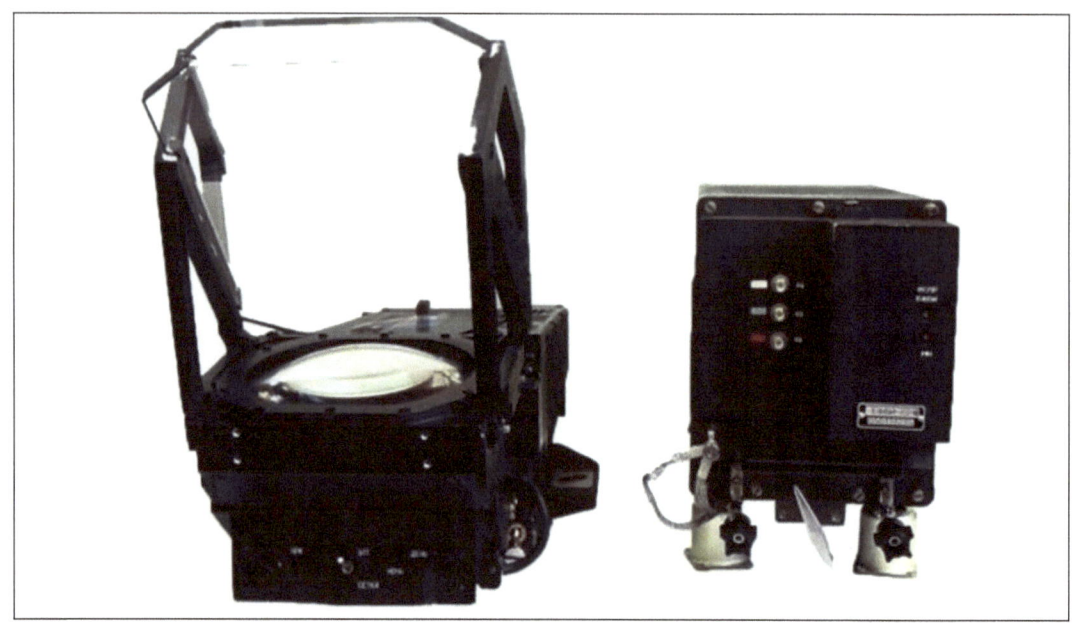

Page 38 and page 39 top: The Su-27K (Su-33) was designed with the ability to be refuelled in flight courtesy of a fully-retractable inflight refuelling probe housed on the port side forward fuselage. This necessitated the OLS complex positioned ahead of the windscreen be offset to starboard. Page 39 bottom and page 40 top: Su-27 variants, including the Su-27K (Su-33), can be equipped with the HUD-31M collimator – HUD (Heads Up Display) – atop the cockpit instrument section just aft of the windscreen. This system, part of the overall Sils-27MV-01 display complex, provides a collimation of various flight/mission data that is available to the pilot without the need to look around the cockpit, which would have negative effects on situational awareness. The system has a full angular field of view, 24° in the vertical plane and 30° in the horizontal plane. Instantaneous field of view is not less than 20-30° at a distance of 400 mm and 18-24° at a distance of 500 mm from the collimator. Above: A USN helicopter approaches the stern of the *Admiral of the Fleet of the Soviet Union, Kuznetsov, with an air wing of* Su-27K, Su-25UTG and Kamov helicopters, during exercise Joint Endeavor on 11 January 1996. US DoD/MODRF

Admiral of the Fleet of the Soviet Union, Kuznetsov with Su-33 air defence fighters, Su-25UTG deck trainers and Ka-27 variant helicopters on deck. Above: Looking like a conventional aircraft carrier, this appearance belied the *Kuznetsov* true capabilities, which was that of a large cruiser/aircraft carrier hybrid featuring a potent all-round anti-air, anti-surface and anti-sub-surface warfare capability. Nevskoe Design Bureau

Project 1143.5 *Admiral of the Fleet of the Soviet Union, Kuznetsov* Aircraft Carrying Heavy Cruiser specification – data furnished by PJSC Nevskoe Design Bureau and MODRF

Displacement: 43,220 tons normal and 55,000 tons, full
Length overall: 273.1 m
Beam overall: 51.3 m
Mean draught at full displacement: 9.3 m (PJSC Nevskoe), 9.14 m (MODRF)
Main propulsion plant: 8 main boilers, 4 MTGA steam turbines, each rated at 4 x 50,000 *hp.*, driving 4 shafts
Speed: 31 knots (PJSC Nevskoe), 29 knots (MODRF)
Range at economic speed of 18 knots: 9914 km (PJSC Nevskoe) 13679 km (MODRF)
Air group: Aircraft, 12 x Su-33 and or MiG-29KR/KUBR and 24 x Ka-27/31 helicopter
Armament: 24 x vertical launch tubes for Tor-M1 derived 9K330 SAM (Surface to Air Missiles) in four six cell launchers; 6 x Kashtan-M SAM/gun complex, each with 32 x 9M311-K missiles and 2,000 rounds of 30 mm ammunition; 6 x AK-630M 6-barrel 30 mm cannon; Granite complex with 12 x P-700 cruise missiles; BOA-1M (RKPTZ-1M) anti-sub-surface rocket system, which has a primary function of defeating torpedoes launched at the host vessel, but can also be used effectively against submarines
Crew: 1,960 persons

Su-25UTG – A development of the Su-25UB ground attack conversion trainer, the naval specific Su-25UTG, was developed as a conversion trainer for pilots transitioning to Su-27K deck operations. As it was prepared for its maiden flight in T-8UTG configuration, the Su-25UB had all of the operational attack and weapon systems removed and an arrestor-hook was installed in line with the design role – to train naval fixed wing aircraft pilots in the art of take-off and arrested landing on an aircraft carrier deck. Sukhoi Design Bureau test pilot I.V. Votintsev took the T-8UTG-1 (Su-25UTG-1) prototype aloft on its maiden flight on 1 September 1988 (conflicting documentation from Sukhoi also provides the date as 24 February 1988, apparently erroneous) (Sukhoi). The factory flight test phase of the Su-25UTG program commenced at the Nikta complex at Saki, Crimea, on 5 September 1988 and the T-8UTG-1 conducted its first arrested landing on the Project 1143.5 ACHC on 1 November 1989 (pilot, I.V. Votintsev and FRI test navigator V.A. Krutov) (Sukhoi). Testing of the Su-25UTG (T-8UTG-1) was completed at the Nikta complex on 11 February 1990. The Su-25UTG entered serial production in 1991, a small number of such aircraft being delivered to Soviet and later Russian Federation naval aviation 279th SFAR (Separate Fighter Aircraft Regiment) of the Northern Fleet, remaining in service in 2019 (Sukhoi).

Su-33 (Su-27K) operating in Northern Waters. Russian Federation Presidential Press and Information Office

Su-33. (UAC)

Serial production of the Su-27K, which was allocated the NATO (North Atlantic Treaty Organisation) reporting name 'Flanker' D, commenced at Komsomolsk-on-Amur in 1989 and the first such aircraft conducted its maiden flight on 17 February 1990 (pilot, I.V. Votintsev). Serial production of the Su-27K ended in 1993. Recent documentation released by Sukhoi states that 34 Su-27K aircraft were built (Sukhoi). This may be an error, but it can be stated with confidence that no less than 24 serial production aircraft and the two prototypes were built, along with the full-scale engineering mock-up.

Official Su-27K State Joint Tests, which had commenced on 25 March 1991, ended in 1994 (Sukhoi). By this time the Soviet Union had been dissolved into a Commonwealth of Independent States, the new Russian Federation taking on-board the naval Su-27 program. Su-27K's were delivered to the 279th SFAR (Separate Fighter Aircraft Regiment) of Russian Naval Aviation in April 1993, with ~24 aircraft delivered by August 1994. The 279th worked up on the aircraft during the period 1993-1995. The Project 1143.5 ACHC *Admiral of the Fleet of the Soviet Union, Kuznetsov* put to sea with a small air group of Su-27K and Su-25UTG aircraft on 21 May 1994 (Sukhoi) as part of this working-up training phase. With considerable training phases completed, the 279th SFAR embarked on the *Kuznetsov* for its maiden long-range operational training voyage, which was conducted between December 1995 and March 1996 (MODRF & Sukhoi). Just over two years later, on 31 August 1998, the Su-27K was officially adopted for service with the Russian Federation Naval Aviation under the new designation Su-33 (MODRF & Sukhoi).

Top: A Su-33, Red 87, is positioned for take-off from the *Admiral Kuznetsov*. Above: Su-27 Red 68 on the deck of the *Kuznetsov* with the Heavy Missile Cruiser *Peter the Great* in the background. KnAAPO/MODRF

Su-27 deck operations on the *Admiral of the Fleet of the Soviet Union, Kuznetsov*.
Sukhoi

Top: A quartet of Su-33's on the deck parking area of the *Admiral of the Fleet of the Soviet Union, Kuznetsov*. Above: Su-33 Blue 109 positioned on a deck life on the *Admiral Kuznetsov*. Sukhoi

Sukhoi Su-33 specification – data furnished by PJSC Sukhoi

Power plant: 2 x AL-31F3 Series 3 afterburning turbofan engines, each rated at 12500 kg -2% with afterburner
Length: 21.9 m
Wingspan: 14.7 m unfolded and 4.4 m folded for stowage
Height: 5.9 m
Normal take-off weight: 23400 kg with 2 x R-27R1 and 2 x R-73E missiles and 5270 kg of fuel
Maximum take-off weight: 33000 kg
Maximum landing weight: 23000 kg
Maximum internal fuel load: 9400 kg
Maximum approach speed: 240 km/h
Maximum speed at sea level: 1400 km/h without external stores
Maximum speed at upper altitude: 2300 km/h without external stores
Ceiling: 17000 m without external stores
Range without in-flight refuelling: 3000 km
Inflight refuelling system
    maximum flow rate: (at entry pressure 3.5 kg/cm^2): 1100 litres per minute
Take-off run: ~450 m at normal take-off weight (terrestrial surface) and 105 from Project 1143.5 aircraft carrier deck
Landing run with braking parachute: ~620 m at normal landing weight (terrestrial surface)
Arrestor assisted landing distance: 90 m on Project 1143.5 aircraft carrier
Load limit: +9 g (conflicting Sukhoi documentation states +8 g, this being the operational load limit, not the maximum without override)
Crew: 1
Fire control System: weapons system based around the RLPK-27 weapon control system, featuring a powerful N001 pulse-Doppler search, track and targeting radar complex; IRST (Infrared Search and Track) and laser rangefinder, optical search and track station; helmet mounted target designator; IFF (Identification Friend or Foe) interrogator; unbiased monitoring system and a wide-angle HUD (Heads Up Display)
Flight navigation system: altitude and heading reference system; radio technical system for short range navigation, landing approach and landing of ship-based aircraft; Doppler navigator; GPS (Global Positioning System); international navigation system
Marker radio receiver; remote control system; IFF transponder
Electronic Counter Measures suite: Radar warning receiver; chaff and flare dispenser; radio jamming transmitter (in podded system)
Other avionics include: Communications system; On-board monitoring system; On-board flight data recording device; On-board voice information playback equipment; Emergency equipment system and Aircraft transponder
Maximum ordnance load: 6500 kg
Armament: 1 x GSh-301 30 mm automatic cannon (150 30 mm rounds); R-27R1(ER1), R-27T1(ET1) and R-73E air to air missiles; S-8KOM, S-80M, S-8BM, S-13T, S-13OF, S-25-OFM PU unguided rockets; general purpose unguided bombs of 50, 100, 250 and 500 kg weight class and RBK-500 cluster bombs carried on 12 external stores stations. MODRF data suggests guided missiles, but this is not replicated in Sukhoi data. The MODRF data may refer to a capability planned for a modernisation program flight tested in 2010

Previous page: Su-33 operations at Severomorsk-3 in North West Russia. This page: Su-33 flight operations out of Severomorsk-3 during 2018. MODRF

3

ARMAMENT/STORES OPTIONS

Initially, it was considered that the Su-27K would have a primary fleet air defence role, complementing the Mikoyan MiG-29K, which was being developed simultaneously as a shorter-range multifunctional strike fighter for operation from the planned fleet of Soviet CTOL (Conventional Take-off and Landing) ACHC (Aircraft Carrying Heavy Cruiser) of the Project 1143.5-1143.8. Following the dissolution of the Soviet Union on 25 December 1991, the harsh economic climate dictated that the new Russian Federation ACHC and naval aircraft programs would be considerably scaled back. It had become clear that, at best, only one of the planned ACHC, the Project 1143.5, would be procured by the Russian Navy. It was equally clear that the Russian Navy could only pursue the procurement of a single fighter aircraft type to serve on the deck of the ship, now named *Admiral of the Fleet of the Soviet Union, Kuznetsov* (formerly the *Tbilisi*), with the Su-27K being selected over the arguably more versatile, but shorter ranged and less capable in the long-range interception role, MiG-29K. While the decision to procure the Su-27K instead of the MiG-29K was widely criticised at the time of implementation in the early 1990's, and in the more than quarter of a century since, it has to be considered that, as the Project 1143.5 dual primary roles – provision of air defence for Soviet and later Russian anti-submarine warfare assets and provision of an anti-submarine warfare role proper, then this decision was the correct one – the Su-27K having more potential for development as an air defence fighter/interceptor than the smaller MiG-29K. With the cancellation of the MiG-29K, it was considered that perhaps the Su-27K would be developed as a multi-role aircraft based on the Su-27M then under development as a multifunctional fighter developed from the Su-27S. Circumstantial evidence used to support this premise was the fact that the aircraft was displayed alongside advanced precision guided air to surface weapon such as the Kh-35 ASM (Anti-Ship Missile) and Kh-31A/P ASM/ARM (Anti-Radiation Missile). However, by 1993, it was becoming clear that the Su-27K was little more than a naval version of the standard Su-27S air superiority fighter, albeit with naval specific capability enhancements and the ability to refuel in flight, the expected enhanced multifunctional development never being fully realised due to the poor economic conditions that prevailed in the Russian Federation in the first decade following the dissolution of the Soviet Union.

The armament options for the Su-33 (the Su-27K was adopted for service as the Su-33 on 31 August 1998) were along the lines of that in place for the Su-27S – primarily medium-range and short-range guided air to air missiles to facilitate the interception of NATO (North Atlantic Treaty Organisation) maritime patrol/ASW (Anti-Submarine Warfare) aircraft and, if required, tactical combat aircraft. For the secondary air to surface mission the Su-33, as was the case with the Su-27S, could employ a diversity of unguided air to surface rockets and unguided bombs.

A Su-33, configured with R-27R1/ER1 series medium-range semi-active radar homing and R-73E short-range infrared homing air to air missiles, approaches the stern of the *Admiral of the Fleet of the Soviet Union, Kuznetsov*. Sukhoi

The Su-33 fixed armament consisted of a GSh-301 30 mm automatic cannon on the starboard side fuselage, carried over from the Su-27S, as was the primary air to air armament of medium range R-27R1(ER1) SARH (Semi-Active Radar Homing), R-27T1(ET1) medium range IR (Infrared) homing and R-73E short range infrared homing air to air missiles. The guided air to air and unguided air to surface munitions were carried on twelve suspension stations, two more than the Su-27S.

The 30 mm calibre GSh-301, which weighed 50 kg (gun weight), featured an independent water-evaporating system to cool the barrel during operation, shock-less 30 mm round chambering and gas powered extraction of expended shell casings. The cannon fired GSh-6-30 30 mm rounds (weight of round is 0.832 kg, of which the projectile weighs 0.39 kg) with a rate of fire of 1500-1800 rounds per minute at a muzzle velocity of 860 metres per second (KBP Tula).

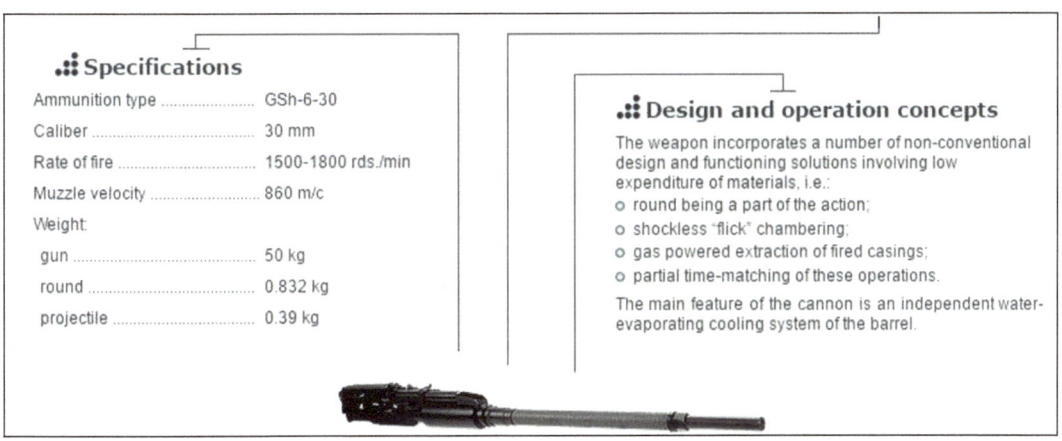

Top: Diagram depicting the key characteristics of the GSh-301 30 mm automatic cannon. Centre: R-27ER1 medium-range radar guided air to air missile. Above: Aviation Trigger APU-470 launcher. KBP Tula/GosMKB Vympel

Up to six R-27R1(ER1) missiles can be carried by the Su-33 – two on the centre fuselage stations, two on the engine trunk stations and one on each of the inner wing stations – launched from Aviation Trigger APU-470 launchers (GosMKB Vympel). Two R-27T1(ET1) can be carried on the inner wing stations in place of two of the R-27R1(ER1) missiles.

Entering service in the mid-1980's as the primary air to air armament of the Su-27S and MiG-29, the Vympel (TMC) R-27 medium-range missile variants in service in 2019 are more capable updates of the R-27, of which a whole family of variants was produced, including the R-27R1 (NATO reporting name AA-10 'Alamo' A) with SARH guidance and the R-27T1 ('Alamo' B) with IR guidance. Longer range variants were also developed – R-27ER1 SARH variant and R-27ET1 passive infrared homing variant. These missiles, 'Alamo' C and 'Alamo' D respectively, are fitted with a boost sustain motor to extend engagement range (GosMKB Vympel & TMC).

An R-27R1/ER1 series radar guided air to air missile carried on the starboard intermediate wing station of a Su-33 during operations to support the Russian mission in the Syrian Arab Republic in late 2016/early 2017. Above: R-27T1/ET1 series infrared guided medium range air to air missile. MODRF/GosMKB Vympel

The R-27ER1 has a length of 4.775 m, diameter 0.26 m at solid rocket motor section and 0.23 m at control unit section, wing span of 0.803 m and control plane span of 0.972 m. The R-27ET1 dimensions are the same as those for the R-27ER1 with the exception of length, which, at 4.49 m, is slightly reduced. The R-27ER1 has a launch weight of 350 kg whilst the R-27ET1 launch weight, at 343 kg, is slightly lower. Missile flight speed is Mach 4, the R-27ER1 having an engagement range of 60 to 62.5 km against a fighter aircraft size target and up to 100 km when used against larger targets such as an AWACS (Airborne Warning and Control System) platform. The infrared guided R-27ET1 has an engagement range of 80 km against a target in the forward hemisphere. Both variants are armed with a 39 kg expanding rod warhead (GosMKB Vympel/TMC).

A Su-33 is positioned for launch from the *Admiral of the Fleet of the Soviet Union, Kuznetsov*. The aircraft is configured with R-27R1/ER1 series missiles on the intermediate wing stations, R-73E IR guided missiles on the outer wing stations and radio jamming transmitter countermeasures pods on the wingtip stations. MODRF

Complementing the infrared guided R-27T1(ET1) is the smaller, shorter range, but very agile, Vympel (TMC) R-73E infrared homing missile, six of which can be carried, one on each of the inner, intermediate and outer wing stations. The R-73E was a generation ahead of its rivals when it entered service in the 1980's, comparable systems being fielded by NATO air arms only in the first decade of the twenty first century.

The R-73 was developed with high agility as a design driver, augmented by the ability of the pilot of the host aircraft, be it an Su-27 or MiG-29 derivative, to cue the weapon to a target at up to 60° off-boresight via the HPS (Helmet Pointing System) or the twenty first century HMTDS (Helmet Mounted Target Designation System). A High level of manoeuvrability was achieved by a combination of a number of design traits – four forward control fins, elevators attached to the rear fins, which are fixed, and deflector vanes positioned in the nozzle of the rocket engine (TMC).

The R-73E, which is carried on and launched from Aviation Trigger P-72-1D series launchers, has a length of 2.9 m, diameter 0.17 m, wing span 0.51 m and a control plane span of 0.38 m, launch weight being 105 kg. The missile, which has a longer reach than most western equivalents, has a maximum engagement range of 30 km against a head-on target and a minimum engagement range of 0.3 km against a tail-on target manoeuvring at up to 12 g. The missile can be launched at altitudes from 0.02 km up to 20 km, the all-aspect passive infrared seeker head guiding the missile to the target, which would then be destroyed by the 8 kg expanding rod warhead (TMC).

The R-73E (top) is the baseline short-range IR guided air to air missile in service with the Su-33. The R-7E is carried on and launched from Aviation Trigger P-72-1D series launchers (above). GosMKB Vympel

The Su-33 secondary air to surface capability was developed along the lines of that developed for the Su-27S. This secondary ground attack capability was proven on 3 October 1980 when K-27 unguided rockets were launched from the T-10-4 (pilot, V.S. Ilyushin) (Sukhoi). Like the Su-27S, the Su-33 can operate with several distinct types of unguided rocket armament options, including a maximum of 80 x 80 mm S-80KOM/Ts-8BM carried in B8M1 rocket pods, each of which contain twenty rockets, which can be launched singly or in salvo fire under environmental conditions of ambient temperatures ±60° Centigrade. The B8M1 rocket pod, which can be carried on the inner wing stations, can be substituted by the B13L pod containing 5 x 122 mm S-13T unguided rockets, a maximum of 20 of which could be carried, five in each of four pods. Like the B8M1 pod, the B13L can launch its rockets singly or in salvo under the same environmental operating conditions. The B8M1 and B13L are carried on BD3-USK-B beam holders (GosMKB Vympel). An alternative armament option is the 266 mm S-25, S-250OFM-PU, four of which could be carried on the same stations as the B8M1 and B13L rocket pods. KnAAPO documentation shows that up to eight of the P-50T weapons can be carried on the inner wing stations (two each), fuselage centre station and engine intake stations.

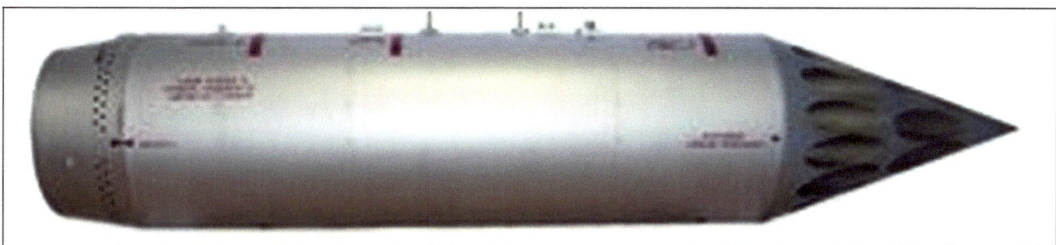

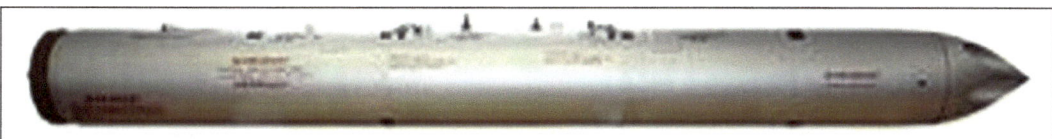

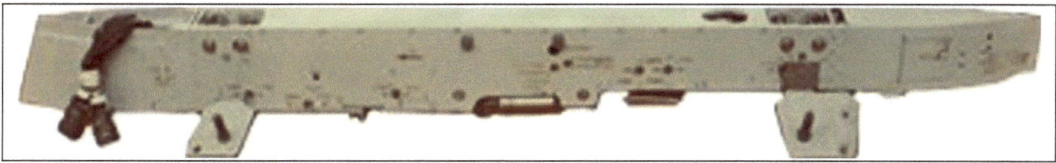

B8M1 rocket pod (top) and B13L rocket pod (centre), which are carried on the BD3-USK-B beam holder (above). GosMKB Vympel

Although not a standard equipment fit, the Su-33, like the Su-27S, can be equipped with the MBD3-U6-68 multi-lock girder holder. This is basically a multiple ejector bomb rack for the carriage of six 250 kg weight class bombs (GosMKB Vympel). Bomb load outs can include a maximum of 32 x OFAB-100-120 general purpose bombs, up to 28 x FAB-250 (OFAB-250-270), general purpose bombs, RBK-250 T.D. or 500 kg class weapons – FAB-500, RBK-500 or BetAB-500 general purpose bombs, up to eight of which can be carried – two on each of the inner wing stations, two on fuselage centre stations and one on each of the intake stations (MODRF).

In the second half of the second decade of the twenty first century the Ministry of Defence of the Russian Federation has circulated documentation that states, emphatically, that the X-41 Moskit and P-800 Onyx derivative weapons are available for operations from the Su-33 (MODRF). This seems unlikely to be standard weapon fits, but it is possible that the limited capability upgrade tested earlier in the 2010's decade included clearance of such a capability.

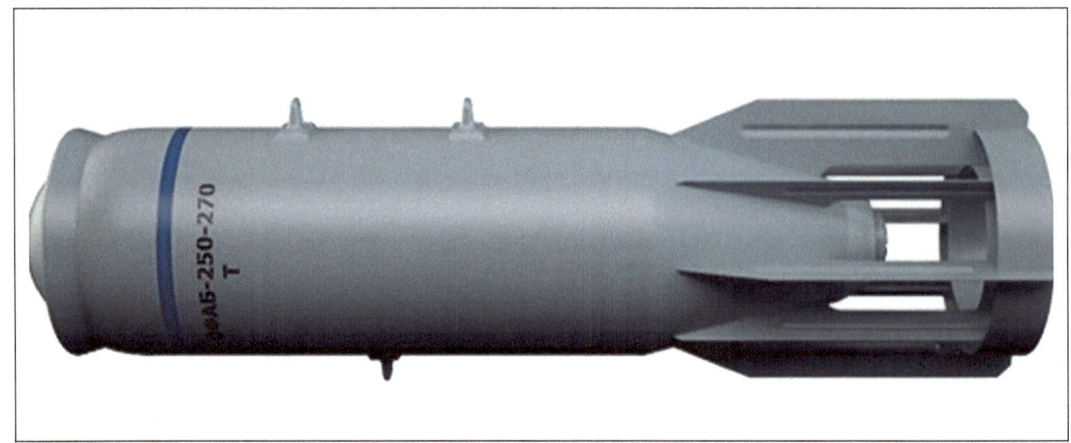

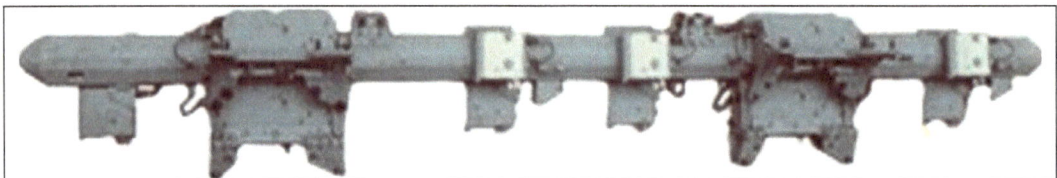

OFAB-250 250 kg bomb (top) and the MBD3-U6-68 multi-lock girder holder (upper centre). Mock-up of an ASM-MSS (X-41) anti-ship cruise missile with an Su-27K (Su-33) in the background, circa 1990's (lower centre). Above: This diagram depicts the Moskit-E surface launched derivative of the X-41. GosMKB Vympel/Rosoboronexport/Almaz

Although recent Ministry of Defence of the Russian Federation documentation states that the X-41 is an armament option for the Su-33, there is no evidence to suggest it is in widespread service. This artwork depicts an Su-33 with a non-standard load-out of six R-27 series air to air missiles, four R-73E air to air missiles and a single X-41 located on the fuselage underside. KnAAPO

The oft quoted ability of the Su-33 to operate with an external fuel tank, notably a 1500 litre unit to be carried on the centreline station, is not supported by Sukhoi and MODRF documentation, and is not considered an operational equipment fit. Range can be further extended through in-flight refuelling for which the Su-33 is equipped with a GPT nozzle assembly mounted on a retractable refuelling probe located on the port side forward fuselage. The Su-33 can be refueled in the air by dedicated airborne tanker aircraft, such as the Ilyushin Il-78M or by tactical size aircraft such as an Su-33 or Su-27UB equipped with a self-contained УПАЗ-1К (UPAZ-1K) unified aerial refueling pod system developed by JSC RD&PE Zvezda. The standard UPAZ pod employs a two-stage centrifugal pump with a ram-air turbine to power the fuel transfer process at a maximum flow rate of 2900 litres per minute. The UPAZ-1K has a standard flow rate up to 2300 litres per minute courtesy of a 52 mm diameter, 26 m length transfer hose (this is the maximum length of the hose that is deployed into the airflow) (Zvezda).

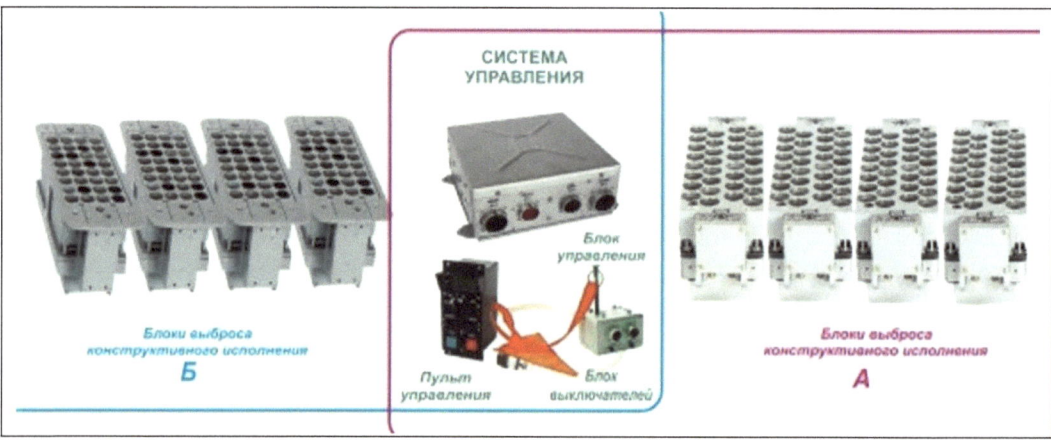

Previous page bottom and this page top: The Su-33 can be refuelled in flight by long-range airborne tanker aircraft or by tactical combat size aircraft configured with the УПАЗ-1К (UPAZ-1K) unified aerial refueling pod system. A Su-33 is refuelled by an Su-27UB development aircraft equipped with the UPAZ-1K. **Above:** UV-26M self-defence countermeasures dispenser suite. MODRF/Zvezda

The Su-33 may be equipped with passive interference devices along the lines of the UV-30MK emission device, the design function of which is to protect the host aircraft from guided missile threats by 'jamming their guidance systems and actuators in the optical and radio bands of electromagnetic waves' (GosMKB Vympel).

4

SYRIAN DEPLOYMENT, 2016-2017

In late 2016, the *Admiral of the Fleet of the Soviet Union, Kuznetsov* embarked upon an operational deployment that would take the vessel and its attendant task group to the Eastern Mediterranean Sea. In this region the *Kuznetsov* battle group joined the Russian Federation effort in support of Syrian Arab Republic government forces in the fight against ISIS (Islamic State) and other opposition groups that had, since 2011, attempted a complete take-over of Syria, throwing the country into violent turmoil. In addition, the air group would be a dissuader against the threat of NATO (North Atlantic Treaty Organisation) nations advocating using airpower (not under the NATO standard) to support Syrian opposition groups by extending offensive air operations against Syrian government forces opposing ISIS. This was the first combat deployment of the *Kuznetsov* in that it would launch strikes on hostile targets.

In late summer 2015, Syrian government forces had been on the verge of a catastrophic collapse due to pressure from ISIS and other opposition groups, some of the latter being supported militarily and financially by the western dominated anti-ISIS coalition that was, in an ironic twist, playing a large part in militarily supporting ISIS, by threatening Syrian government forces, forcing the latter to make dispositions accordingly. Russia took the decision to intervene militarily in the conflict, commencing with air operations on 30 September 2015. This Russian intervention, which allowed the Syrian government forces to go on the offensive and retake large swathes of territory from ISIS and western supported opposition forces, was reduced in tempo in March 2016. However, in late 2016, western backed opposition groups fighting in Aleppo carved out closer cooperation with the extremists of the Al-Qaeda and ISIS affiliated Al Nusra Front. This led to a stiffening of resistance in Aleppo, the main defence of which was conducted by Al Nusra Front. South of Aleppo, ISIS launched an offensive against Palmyra, which had been liberated by Russian supported Syrian government forces in March 2016. The ISIS offensive recaptured Palmyra, taking advantage of the tactical situation as Syrian government Forces were drawn into the Aleppo battle, the objective being the collapse of the government offensive against Aleppo as well as the capture of ground in and around Palmyra.

The Russian task group that departed from Northern Fleet bases consisted of the Project 1143.5 ACHC (Aircraft Carrying Heavy Cruiser) *Admiral of the Fleet of the Soviet Union, Kuznetsov,* the Nuclear powered Heavy Missile Cruiser, *Pyotr Velikiy* (*Peter the Great*), the Large ASW (Anti-Submarine Warfare) ships *Severomorsk* and *Vice-Admiral Kulakov* and four support vessels. This task group joined an estimated 10 other Russian ships in the Eastern Mediterranean (MODRF).

The *Kuznetsov* brought with her a wealth of capability, much of which was new to the Russian campaign in Syria. This included an in-flight refueling capability for strike aircraft (it is unclear if this was employed) and a rotary winged AEW (Airborne Early Warning) capability courtesy of the Ka-31 helicopter (this capability is assumed and, if present, would have been restricted to fleet protection duties – the Russian Aerospace Group bases in Syria operated a limited AWACS (Airborne Warning & Control) capability with at an Ilyushin A-50/U deployed on a rotational basis). Enhancements to existing capabilities in the Syrian theatre included an enhanced scout/attack helicopter capability, air defence fighters and multirole strike fighters, as well as additional air defence capability for the naval presence, courtesy of *Kuznetsov's* integral air defence system and electronic warfare capabilities. The Russian surface to surface anti-ship capability was significantly enhanced through *Kuznetsov's* twelve P-700 Granit supersonic anti-ship cruise missiles, adding to the anti-ship missiles on the *Peter the Great* and additional Russian surface assets already in theatre – these systems being important politically as at that time misguided voices within western politics were advocating using shipborne surface to air missile systems on western coalition warships in the Eastern Mediterranean Sea to engage and shoot down Syrian aircraft, which endanger Syrian government and Russian forces combating ISIS and AL Nusra Front. The presence of such a powerful Russian anti-ship capability within her task group was a less than subtle message that Russia was prepared to counter all threats to her air operations over Syria.

The Kuznetsov air group consisted of a mix of Ka-27PL ASW and Ka-27PS search and rescue helicopters, Ka-31 AEW helicopters (unconfirmed), Su-33 fleet air defence fighters, MiG-29KR (and possibly KUBR) multidimensional strike fighters and a small group of Ka-52K scout/attack helicopters. Although details of the *Kuznetsov* group strike operations are sparse, the Chief of the General Staff of the Russian Armed Forces, General of the Army, Valery Geriasimov, confirmed that the *Kuznetsov* Groups aviation assets had been involved in operations leading to the 'liberation of Aleppo' (MODRF). Operations were also, it is understood, flown against ISIS targets in other parts of Syria. Missions were flown over Syria by Su-33, MiG-29KR/KUBR and the small detachment of Ka-52K scout/attack helicopters. In addition, the naval task grouping launched Kalibr cruise missile strikes on opposition targets in Syria on 15/16 November 2016. Details, released by Russia's Northern Fleet Vice Admiral Nikolay Evmenova in early summer 2017 included a sortie total of 420 for the *Kuznetsov* air group. It was noted that 117 of these sorties were flown during the hours of darkness and most of the sortie total was flown in conditions of adverse weather. More than 1,000 targets were struck – command facilities, groupings of enemy forces and fixed fortified fire positions (MODRF).

Su-33

The implementation, from 00.00 hours on 30 December 2016, of a shaky ceasefire, which would lead to peace talks in Astana, Kazakhstan, led to a decision by the Supreme Commander-in-Chief of the Russian Armed Forces to drawdown Russian forces in the Syria region. This included the early termination of the operational deployment of the *Kuznetsov* Group of the Northern Fleet, which was announced on 6 January 2017. The *Kuznetsov* group moved into Northern waters off Norway in late January 2017 and returned to Russia several days later (MODRF).

Su-33 aircraft codes known to have taken part in the operation include Red 62, Red 66, Red 67, Red 71, Red 76, Red 77, Red 78, Red 84, Red 85 and Red 88 (MODRF).

Previous page and this page top: *Admiral of the Fleet of the Soviet Union, Kuznetsov* air wing during operations in support of the Russian air campaign over Syria during November-December 2016. Above: Su-33 of the 279th **SFAR** landing at Severomorsk-3, Northern Russia, in early 2017, having flown off the *Admiral of the Fleet of the Soviet Union, Kuznetsov* on its return from operations off the coast of the Syrian Arab Republic. MODRF

5

RETIREMENT OR MODERNISATION

With the Project 1143.5 ACHC (Aircraft Carrying Heavy Cruiser) *Admiral of the Fleet of the Soviet Union, Kuznetsov* undergoing a major modernisation and not scheduled to re-join the Northern Fleet until 2020-2021, it would have been prudent for Russian naval aviation to have retired the Sukhoi Su-33 in the 2017-2019 timeframe, had that indeed been the intention. However, in the third quarter of 2019, the Su-33 remains in operational service, shore based, within Russian Naval Aviation air assets, alongside the RAC MiG-29KR/KUBR shipborne multifunctional strike fighter (shore based in 2019), shore based MiG-31 long-range interceptor, Su-27S interceptor/fighter, Su-30SM multifunctional strike fighter and the Su-24M shore based strike aircraft.

Retirement of the Su-33 had been speculated following the introduction to service of the MiG-29KR/KUBR in the second half of the second decade of the twenty first century. Going into 2019, information emerged that suggested that far from facing imminent retirement, the Su-33 fleet may well undergo a modernisation program to allow them to remain viable going into the third decade of the twenty first century. A modernised Su-33 had been flight tested at KnAAPO from 5 October 2010 (Sukhoi). For most of the second decade of the twenty first century the modernisation program appeared to be in limbo, with expectation that the ordering of 24 MiG-29KR/KUBR multifunctional strike fighters for Russian naval aviation signalled the impending retirement of the Su-33. However, in 2019 it appears that a modernisation program remains extant. What is less clear is the modernisation substance and scope, particularly in regard to the sensor suite, assuming it proceeds to serial implementation. It can be speculated that the modernisation could incorporate either a variation of the Tikhomirov Irbis or Bars radar complexes incorporated in the Su-35S and Su-30SM respectively. However, another, less costly and more realistic option would be an enhancement of the existing radar complex to bring it up to the standard fitted in the Su-27SM(3) and Su-30M2 strike fighters delivered to the Russian Air Force in 2011. This would add to small enhancements to the equipment fit implemented over the past decade or so.

Depiction of an unrealised advanced Su-33 derivative launching an air launched cruise missile. KnAAPO

The main driving force behind the Su-27SM/SKM updates were aimed at improving the designs multirole capabilities, particularly in regard to the carriage and employment of precision guided air to surface munitions. For the Su-30M2 and Su-27SM(3) designs, enhancements to the Tikhomirov NIIP N001 radar system allowed the application of new advanced weapons such as the RVV-AE active radar guided air to air missile and precision guided air to surface munitions (Sukhoi). While the primary role of the Su-27SM(3) remained that of an air superiority fighter aircraft the primary mission of the Su-30M2 was that of a long-range strike fighter.

The avionics and fire control system of the Su-27SM(3) was along the lines of those introduced on the Su-27SM, although some systems apparently featured enhancements over those installed in the SM modernisation. Although outdated by $4^{th}++$ or $5^{th}+$ generation standards, the Su-27SM(3) cockpit standard is half a generation ahead of the Su-27S/SK and Su-33. The cockpit, which is dominated by the SILS-27M HUD (Heads Up Display) in front of the windscreen (integrated with a Berkt-1 video recording unit), featured an open architecture avionics suite developed by RPKB Ramenskoye Design Bureau. This apparently included an SUV-P-E cockpit & fire control management system, which incorporated a BTsVM-486-2M, or equivalent, computer, two 152 mm x 208 mm class MFI-10-6M colour MFDS (Multi-Function Display Screen) and a MFPI-6 colour multifunctional display panel with several push buttons. The displays can replicate all relevant targeting, weapons, fuel, flight and navigational data – these forming the major elements of the cockpit data management system – a number of traditional dial style cockpit controls being retained, most of which are for back-up purposes only. Other systems incorporated in the Su-27SM(3) include the secure radio – UHF and VHF communications system – compatible with modern ground based aerial communications systems such as the NKVS-27, and a GPS satellite navigation system, apparently an A-737-010 that is compatible with the Russian GLONASS and American NAVSTAR systems. Lacking, in the initial Su-27SM(3) release, an Su-33 modernisation may incorporate a variation of the BINS-SP-2 strap down INS (Inertial Navigation System), which would allow the aircraft to navigate accurately even in the absence of GPS signals, ground based or offshore navigational data.

The cockpit layout in the Su-27SKM demonstrator, Black 305, is dominated by the HUD, two colour MFDS and the colour multifunction panel. This is representative of the Su-27SM, but the Su-27SM(3) is stated to feature four multifunction displays. Any Su-33 modernisation may be more representative of the Su-27SM(3). Sukhoi

An enhanced variant of the SUU-VE installed in the Su-30MKK, designated SUU-VEP, was developed for the Su-30MK2, this also being the standard selected for the Su-27SM/SKM. The SUU-VEP consists of the RLPK-27VEP (Article N001VEP) pulse-Doppler fire control radar, operating in high, medium and low frequencies; OEPS-27MK (Article 31E-MK) Optical Electronic Sighting System, incorporating the OLS-27MK (Article 52Sh) OLS (Optical Location Station); SURA-K HMTDS (Helmet Mounted Target Designation System) (other HMTDS can be specified), SILS-27M HUD (Heads up Display) and the 6231R IFF (Identification Friend or Foe) interrogator (Tikhomirov).

Although details of the Su-33 update test flown in 2010 are sparse, it is thought that this was based on the equipment specified for the Su-27SM(3) (above) (unconfirmed). Twelve Su-27SM(3) multifunctional fighters were procured by the Russian Federation Air Force (Aerospace forces from 2015), the last being delivered in December 2011. Sukhoi

The N001VEP can detect and track targets in a zone of ±60° in azimuth and -55° - +60° in elevation. The system can process ten targets in track while scan mode and engage two targets simultaneously. In close combat mode, search and lock-on zone is ± 2° in azimuth and -10° to +50° in elevation. Detection range for a fighter aircraft size target with a RCS=3 m^2, with 0.5 probability, is put at no less than 100 km (in long range detection mode the range can be increased to 150 km) in look-up mode in forward hemisphere. Effective range in look-up mode in tail hemisphere is ~40 km and ~80 km for look down in forward hemisphere, reducing to ~35 km for look down in tail hemisphere. An aircraft carrier size vessel with a radar cross section of 50000 m^2 can be detected at rages out to ~350 km, and a destroyer size vessel with a cross section of 10000 m^2 can be detected at ranges of ~250 km (Tikhomirov).

The OEPS-27MK (Item 31E-MK) Optical Electronic Sight System, developed by the UMAZ (Urals Opto-mechanical plant) and specified for the Su-27SM(3), combines an IRST (Infrared Search and Track) and laser illumination channel capability. The OLS element of the system consists of the OLS-27MK (Article 52Sh), which provides the host aircraft with a passive (radar silent – non emitting radar emissions) detection, tracking and engagement capability, reducing overall vulnerability to enemy direct and indirect detection, tracking and engagement systems and countermeasures – such systems also proving to be effective at countering radar return reduction (stealth) technology (Tikhomirov).

Su-33

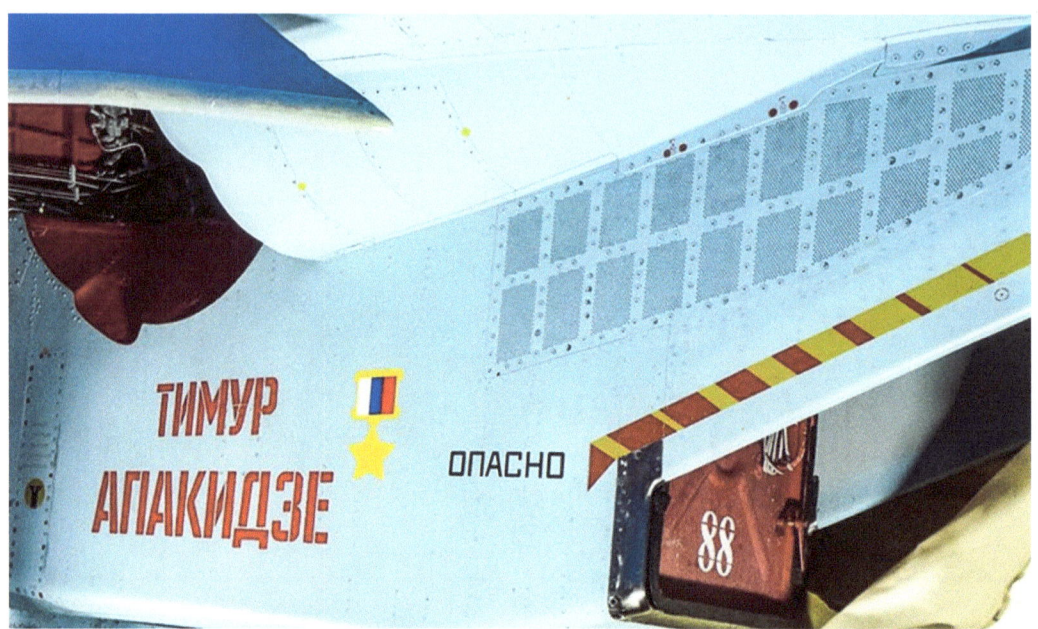

Previous page top: MODRF data concerning this photograph states a Su-33 landing on the deck of the *Admiral of the Fleet of the Soviet Union, Kuznetsov* in June 2018, but this may be 2017. Previous page bottom and this page: In late 2018, the honorary names *Timur Apakidze* and *Feoktist Matkovsky* were assigned to Su-33's of the Northern Fleet. MODRF

The OLS, which can also be employed in conjunction with the radar, with which it is integrated, features an in azimuth tracking zone of ±- 60° and -15 to +60° in elevation. This system features a 60° in azimuth and 10° in elevation field of view and search; a 20° in azimuth and 5° in elevation small field of view and search; close combat area (Vertical' mode) 3 x -15° to + 60° and Lock-on area 3° x 3°. Released data shows that against an air target in infrared contrast in the tail on aspect for a target in the class of a Sukhoi Su-15 interceptor operating without afterburner 'PMFU)' the OLS-27MK system has a detection range of 'no less than 30 km'; a target in the class of the RAC MiG-25 at high altitude in the forward aspect in afterburner flying at a speed of at least Mach 2.0 can be detected at 'no less than 90 km and against an airborne target in the RAC MiG-21 class the laser rangefinder can be operated at ranges up to 8 km and 0.3 to 10 km against ground targets (Tikhomirov).

Su-33 operating from Severmorsk-3 airbase in the Murmansk Region of North West Russia. MODRF

The self-defence suite includes an L-150 Pastel RWR (Radar Warning Receiver) ELINT (Electronic Intelligence) system, which, as well as alerting the pilot to threat radar systems, can provide targeting information to Kh-31P anti-radiation missiles in the defence suppression role, should such a weapon capability be incorporated. In its primary function the system provides a detection (including in track-while scan mode) and direction finding capability and can prioritise threat radar providing the pilot with relative information on which systems pose the most immediate threat, an audible alarm sounding when the host aircraft has been illuminated by a threat radar or the seeker head of a semi-active or active radar guided missile, the radiation emissions of which are detected when the systems are actively operating in target acquisition, tracking and illumination mode. The system, which weighs 45 kg (excluding the display), operates in the 2-18 GHz frequency bands against quasi-continuous, continuous and pulse radar signals with a location accuracy of 3-10°.

The suite also includes decoy systems, UV-30MK chaff dispenser, which can jam 'guidance systems and executive mechanisms with passive countermeasures effective in optical and radar frequency bands,' and dispense flares to counter infrared guided missiles (TMC). A modernised Su-33 may be capable of employing advanced wingtip mounted ECM (Electronic Counter Measures) systems such as the Khbiny-U system carried by the Su-30SM.

Digital artist rendering of a national Novator 3M-54-AE supersonic air launched cruise missile being launched from a Su-33. Novator

The Su-27SM/SKM variants can be equipped with a modern armament management system, a variation of which could be incorporated into a modernised Su-33. The complex equipping the Su-27SM is apparently an SUO-30PKR-E unit integrated with a WCS-VEP (Sh101VEP) weapons control system, which provision for the operation of a wide diversity of guided and unguided air to air and air to surface weapons. Particular weapons capability enhancements over the unmodernised Su-33 include the ability to carry and launch up to six RVV-AE active radar guided medium range air to air missiles from the AKU-170E ejection device, one on each of the inner wing stations, one on each of the engine trunk stations and two carried in tandem on the centre fuselage stations. Sukhoi documentation confirms that the Su-33 fleet is being cleared for use with the RVV-AE and that updates to the 'radar sighting system' and 'weapon control system' were incorporated (Sukhoi). Operational parameters of the RVV-AE include a minimum engagement range of 0.3 km in the rear hemisphere and a maximum range of 80 km in the forward hemisphere, the missile reaching speeds of Mach 4 and able to engage targets manoeuvring at up to 12 g at altitudes from 0.2 km up to 25 km (TMC).

As of 2019 the electronic suite for the Su-33 included the weapon control system: radar sighting system (updated), optical electronic sighting system, optical location station, helmet targeting system, Requestor of state recognition system and single display system; Satellite navigation system; Information complex vertical and course; Radio navigation system; Automatic control system; Radio altimeter; Air signal system; Limit signal system; Respondent of state identification system; Complex of communications facilities, Coherent radio station MV-UHF ranges, HF (High Frequency) radio communications station and Telecode communications terminal equipment; Electronic countermeasures; Radiation Warning Station; Interference Station (in container (pod); Device for resetting dipole reflectors and false thermal targets; Control and registration system; Generalised integrated crew monitoring and warning System; Flight recording equipment; Alarm system; Aircraft respondent and Command guidance equipment (Sukhoi).

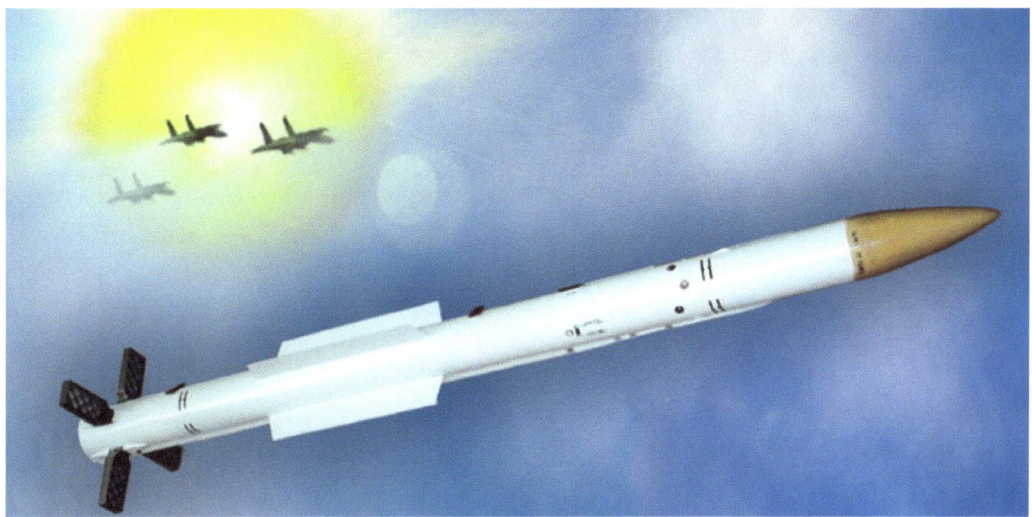

Top: RVV-AE medium-range active radar guided air to air missile in service with the Russian Federation. Above: Artist rendering showing a notional Su-33 derivative armed with four X-31A anti-ship missiles, R-27ER1 and R-73E air to air missiles. KnAAPO

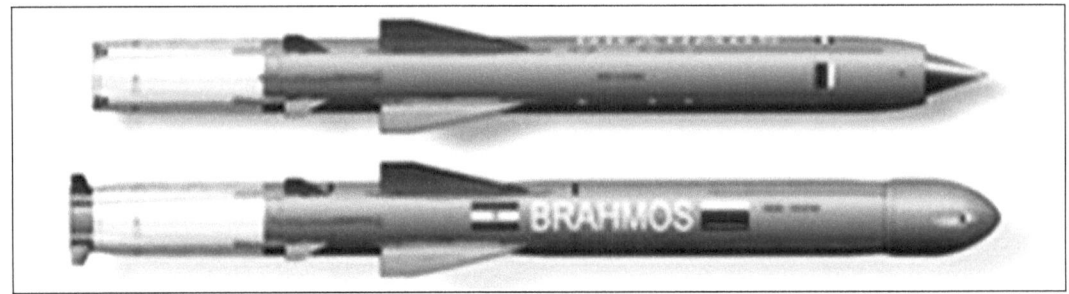

P-800 Onyx supersonic anti-ship missile (upper) and Indian-Russian Brahmos development (lower). The P-800 derivative is stated by the MODRF to be an armament option for the Su-33. GosMKB Vympel/Granit-electron

The updates inherent in the Su-27SM(3)/Su-30M2 provision for the carriage and deployment of a number of advanced air to surface weapon options. Up to four Kh-31A ASM (Anti-Ship Missile) or Kh-31P anti-radiation missiles can be carried, one on each of the inner intermediate (Su-27SM(3)) wing stations and one on each of the engine trunk stations. The Kh-31P is cleared on the domestic Su-27SM (apparently since November 2008), but there is a lack of clarity as to whether or not the Kh-31A has been cleared for use on the Su-27SM(3). In regard to the Su-33, an update would most likely provision for the carriage of the Kh-31A variant, up to four of which could be carried and launched from AKU-58A ejection units. These weapons can be launched from altitudes of 100 m to 15000 m at a carrier speed of Mach 0.65 to Mach 1.25, after which it flies to targets between 15 to 110 km away (depending upon launch altitude), at speeds of 1000 m/s (3600 km/h). The target is destroyed by an 87 kg high explosive fragmentation warhead (TMC).

The on-board active-radar homing head of the Kh-31A can designate targets in both pre-and-post launch modes, conduct target acquisition and selection and determines 'target coordinates (range, azimuth, elevation), [and] generation of command signals', which are fed directly to the guidance system (TMC). The Kh-31A can be launched either singly or in salvo in clear and adverse weather conditions in a high threat active jamming environment. Once launched the missile cruises at a speed of 1000 m/s to targets 5 to 70 km distant (against a Destroyer size target), dependant on launch altitude, the target being destroyed or disabled by the 95 kg high explosive warhead (TMC).

There are a number of other advanced precision guided weapon options that may be incorporated into a Su-33 capability update. These may include advanced air to surface missiles, such as the Kh-59MK2, and may allow for the delivery of guided bomb units of the KAB-500Kr(OD) and KAB-1500Kr types, four of the 520 kg weight KAB-500Kr or four of the 370 kg KAB-500OD weapons able to be carried on the same stations as employed for the Kh-31 missiles, but only one of the larger 1525 kg weight KAB-1500Kr weapons able to be carried across fuselage centre stations. The KAB-500 class weapons can be released from altitudes of 0.5 to 5 km at carrier speeds of 550 to 1100 km/h. Launch parameters for the KAB-1500Kr are 1 to 8 km altitude and 550 to 1100 km/h carrier speed (TMC).

Although Su-33 updates are primarily focussed on sensor/avionics/weapons enhancements to improve the multifunctional capability of the design, it is possible that a naval specific derivative of the uprated MMPP Salut AL-31F-1M (Series 42) engine, introduced on the second contract for upgrades of the Su-27S to Su-27SM standard, could be incorporated into a modernised Su-33. Such engines have an afterburning rating of 13500 kgf, some 1000 kgf higher than the AL-31F3 of the Su-33. Another potential engine for a modernised Su-33 would be the AL-41F powering Su-35S multidimensional strike fighters, late production Su-34 multifunctional strike fighters and development examples of Su-57 (T-50) 5th generation multidimensional fighters. However, cost considerations would likely focus attention on overhauling the existing fleet of AL-31F3 engines rather than procurement of a new engine type.

Previous page top: An Su-33 engages afterburner over the Northern Fleet air base at Severomorsk-3 in January 2018. Previous page bottom: The Project 1143.5 Aircraft Carrying Heavy Cruiser *Admiral of the Fleet of the Soviet Union, Kuznetsov* circa 2016-2017 with an air wing of Su-33 fleet air defence fighters, MiG-29KR multifunctional strike fighters and Ka-27/28 helicopters. This page top: An Su-33 at a snow covered Severomorsk-3 in January 2019. Above: In 2019 it is somewhat hazy what the long-term planning holds for the Russian Federation Su-33 fleet – the Sun may be setting on its service life or it may be rising for a revival of the fleet with the rolling introduction of updates to keep that fleet current in the third decade of the twenty first century. MODRF

ADDENDUM

Whilst speculation that a naval specific variant of the Su-27UB was being developed as a two-seat conversion trainer to complement the Su-27K proved unfounded, as did similar speculation about the Su-27IB, Sukhoi had studied a conversion trainer variant of the Su-27K. In the mid-1980's these studies spawned the T-10KU/T-10-KT. Such a design fell by the wayside, but a naval specific conversion trainer variant of the T-10 resurfaced in the 1990's, the T-10-K4 being built as the T-10KUB during 1995-1999. The aircraft conducted its maiden flight on 29 April 1999 crewed by test pilots V.G. Pugachev (commander) and S.N. Melnikov (co-pilot), but this variant did not enter serial production (Sukhoi).

Su-33

Page 77-78: In 1999, Sukhoi flew the Su-33KUB (T-10KUB), which was a side-by-side two seat variant of the Su-33 adapted for aircraft carrier conversion training. This variant did not enter serial production. This page: Two Su-25UTG deck operation trainer aircraft (top) and a Su-25UTG arrestor hook (above) Sukhoi/Ilyushin

The Su-33 serves alongside the MiG-29KR/KUBR shipborne multifunctional fighter (top) and shore based multifunctional fighters in the guise of the Su-30SM (above). MODRF

Su-33

Su-33

Page 81-83: China's People's Liberation Army Navy operates the aircraft carrier *Liaoning*, converted from the incomplete former Soviet Project 1143.6 *Varyag*, which was purchased from the Ukraine. This vessel operates an air wing that included the Shenyang J-15, a Chinese copy of the Su-33. AVIC

GLOSSARY

ACHC	Aircraft Carrying Heavy Cruiser
AEW	Airborne Early Warning
AoA	Angle of Attack
ASW	Anti-Submarine Warfare
AWACS	Airborne Warning and Control System
CCCP	Union of Soviet Socialist Republics
CTOL	Conventional Take-Off and Landing
DoD	Department of Defence
ECM	Electronic Counter Measures
EDCS	Electronic Distance Control System
ELINT	Electronic Intelligence
F	Fighter
FAR	Fighter Aircraft Regiment
FBW	Fly-By-Wire
FCS	Flight Control System
ft.	Feet (unit of measurement)
FX	Fighter Experimental
GHz	Gigahertz
GLONASS	Globanaya Navigozionnaya Sputnikovaya Sistema/Global Navigation Satellite System
GPS	Global Positioning System
HACC	Heavy Aircraft Carrying Cruiser
HF	High Frequency
HMTDS	Helmet Mounted Target Designation Systems
HP	High Pressure
hp	Horse Power
HPS	Helmet Pointing System
HUD	Heads Up Display
IA-PVO	*Istrebitelnaya Aviatsiya Protivo-Vozdushnoy Obstrany*/Air Defence Force
IFF	Identification Friend or Foe
INS	Inertial Navigation System
IRST	Infrared Search and Track
ISIS	Islamic State of Iraq and the Levant (internationally prescribed terrorist organisation)
kg	Kilogram
kgf	Kilogram force
km	Kilometre
km/h	Kilometres per hour
kN	Kilo Newton
KnAAPO	Komsomolsk-on-Amur Aviation Plant (named after Yu.A. Gagarin) a branch of PJSC Aviation Holding Company, Sukhoi

Knots	Nautical Miles per Hour
lb.	Pound (unit of weight)
LERX	Leading Edge Root Extensions
LP	Low Pressure
LR	Laser Rangefinder
m	Metre
m^2	Metres squared
m/s	Meters per second
Mach	1 Mach = the speed of sound (this varies with altitude)
MAI	Ministry of Aviation Industry
MFDS	Multi-Function Display Screen
MiG	Mikoyan
mm	Millimetre
MODRF	Ministry of Defence of the Russian Federation
MRCA	Multi-Role Combat Aircraft
NATO	North Atlantic Treaty Organisation
NAVSTAR	Navigation Satellite Timing and Ranging
OLS	Optical Location Station
PFI	Advanced Frontline Fighter
RAC	Russian Aircraft Corporation
RWR	Radar Warning Receiver
SAM	Surface to Air Missile
SFAR	Separate Fighter Aircraft Regiment
STOVL	Short-Take-Off and Vertical Landing
Su	Sukhoi
TMC	Tactical Missiles Corporation
TsAGI	Central Aerodynamic Institute
UEC	United Engine Corporation
UHF	Ultra-High Frequency
US	United States
USSR	Union of Soviet Socialist Republics
VHF	Very High Frequency
x	Multiplication
±	Plus or minus
~	Approximately equal to (can also be used to mean asymptotically equal)
°	Degree(s)

ABOUT THE AUTHOR

Hugh Harkins FRAS is a historian and author with an extensive research background in astro/geophysics and studies/research in the wider scientific, aeronautic, astronautic and nautical technical and historical fields. He is also involved in research in the field of Scottish history, which formed a significant element of an otherwise scientific undergraduate degree. Hugh has published in excess of sixty books; non-fiction and fiction, writing under his given name as well as utilising several pseudonyms. He has also written for several international magazines, whilst his work has been used as reference for many other projects ranging from the aviation industry, international news corporations and film media to encyclopaedias, museum exhibits and the computer gaming industry. Hugh is a member of the Institute of Physics and is an elected Fellow of the Royal Astronomical Society. He currently resides in his native Scotland. Other titles by the author include:

Russia's Coastal Missile Shield - Bal-E & Bastion Mobile Coastal Cruise Missile Complexes
Iskander - Mobile Tactical Aero-Ballistic/Cruise Missile Complex
Orbital/Fractional Orbit Bombardment System - The Soviet Globalnaya Raketa
Counter-Space Defence Co-Orbital Satellite Fighter
Russia's Strategic Missile Carrier/Bomber Roadmap 2018-2040 – PAK DA, Tu-160M2, Tu-95MSM & Tu-22M3M
Sukhoi T-50/PAK FA - Russia's 5th Generation 'Stealth' Fighter
Sukhoi Su-35S 'Flanker' E - Russia's 4++ Generation Super-Manoeuvrability Fighter
Sukhoi Su-34 'Fullback'
Sukhoi Su-30MKK/MK2/M2 - Russo Kitashiy Striker from Amur
Soviet Mixed Power Experimental Fighter Aircraft – Piston-Liquid Propellant Rocket Engine/Piston-Ramjet/Piston-Pulsejet & Piston-Compressor Jet Engine Designs of the 1940's
MiG-35/D 'Fulcrum' F – Towards the Fifth Generation
Air War over Syria, Tu-160, Tu-95MS & Tu-22M3 - Cruise Missile and Bombing Strikes on Syria, November 2015-February 2016
Sukhoi Su-27SM(3)/SKM
Russian/Soviet Aircraft Carrier & Carrier Aviation Design & Evolution Volume 1 - Seaplane Carriers, Project 71/72, Graf Zeppelin, Project 1123 ASW Cruiser & Project 1143-1143.4 Heavy Aircraft Carrying Cruiser
Light Battle Cruisers and the Second Battle of Heligoland Bight
British Battlecruisers of World War 1 - Operational Log, July 1914-June 1915
Eurofighter Typhoon - Storm over Europe
North American F-108 Rapier - Mach 3 Interceptor
Convair YB-60 - Fort Worth Overcast
Boeing X-36 Tailless Agility Flight Research Aircraft
X-32 - The Boeing Joint Strike Fighter
X-35 - Progenitor to the F-35 Lightning II
X-45 Uninhabited Combat Air Vehicle
Into The Cauldron - The Lancaster MK.I Daylight Raid on Augsburg
Hurricane IIB Combat Log - 151 Wing RAF, North Russia 1941
RAF Meteor Jet Fighters in World War II, an Operational Log
Typhoon IA/B Combat Log - Operation Jubilee, August 1942
Defiant MK.I Combat Log - Fighter Command, May-September 1940
Blenheim MK.IF Combat Log - Fighter Command Day Fighter Sweeps/Night Interceptions, September 1939 - June 1940
Fortress MK.I Combat Log - Bomber Command High Altitude Bombing Operations, July-September 1941

www.ingramcontent.com/pod-product-compliance
Lightning Source LLC
Chambersburg PA
CBHW040058160426
43192CB00003B/107